EVOLVE
INTO YOUR ALL

Create & Live in the 5th Dimension of Love, Joy & Prosperity!

Featuring The Diamond Co-Creative System®

I0558012

Amanda Slade

Published By:
Co-Create Your Success

Disclaimer

The author of this book and its materials do not dispense medical advice or prescribe the use of any tool or technique as a form of treatment for physical, mental, or emotional problems without the advice of a trained health professional, either directly or indirectly. The intent of the author is only to offer information of a general nature to help you, which you can choose to believe what feels right for you in your quest for emotional and mental well-being, optimal health, and spiritual growth. In the event you use any of the information in this book for yourself, which is your right and choice, the author and the publisher assume no responsibility, nor are they held liable for your actions or results.

ISBN: 979-8-9921511-0-7 (Paperback)
ISBN: 979-8-9921511-5-2 (Hardcover)
ISBN: 979-8-9921511-2-1 (E-Book)

Evolve Into Your All is dedicated
to those who seek
to heal the past, enliven their spirit,
and live in the consciousness of Love
so they can thrive and prosper as their True Self.

PRAISES FOR AMANDA SLADE & THE DIAMOND CO-CREATIVE SYSTEM®

I thankfully learned about Amanda Slade and The Diamond Co-Creative System® when I was struggling to overcome a debilitating health challenge and recreate my coaching business. I had been searching for something that would get me past these major obstacles, but nothing spoke to my Soul the way Amanda and the Elevation Codes did.

After a very short time it seemed almost miraculous when my health began to improve by leaps and bounds. I found I was able to be clear and joyfully experience a more Soulfully directed life and business. I absolutely know this would not have been possible without the deeply caring support and expert healing and teaching of Amanda. I highly recommend working with Amanda and the beautiful, amazing Elevation Codes, and participating in any of the powerful programs she offers utilizing The Diamond Co-Creative System®.

– Rachelle Lasater, Transformational Life Coach, CA

I've had the absolute pleasure of working with Amanda Slade in multiple ways — attending her virtual retreats, diving into her programs, and working with her one-on-one. And let me tell you — she is a powerhouse! Amanda is deeply connected to her spiritual guides, which allows her to deliver insights with lightning speed and incredible clarity.

When I was in the process of creating a new program for my business, Amanda helped me cut through the noise and get crystal clear on the format, price point, and marketing strategy — quickly and effortlessly. I walked away with a solid plan and a deep sense of alignment.

Beyond that, learning how to use The Diamond Co-Creative System® has been a total game-changer, not just in my business but in every area of my life. I'm beyond grateful for Amanda's wisdom, guidance, and the way she helps her clients tap into their highest potential!

– Leisa Reid, Speaker Trainer, CA

Working with The Diamond Co-Creative System® and its Elevation Codes has been the most profound transformational journey of my life. Before discovering this System, I lived in my head, doubted my wisdom, and equated service with suffering — now I trust myself implicitly, stand confidently in my heart-centered power, and share my wisdom and spiritual gifts with remarkable ease. *The System provides me with practical tools to heal my relationship with myself and family members, transform my relationship with money, and connect deeply with my Soul's purpose.*

What continues to amaze me is how these tools expand and accelerate the healing and transformation provided through my professional work since I became accredited as a practitioner, coach, and teacher of the System. Healing and shifts for my clients that once took months are now unfolding in a single session.

The Diamond Co-Creative System® didn't just change my life — it revolutionized how I show up in the world, allowing me to flow in financial abundance and service, while remaining deeply anchored in love, peace, and freedom.

– Maurine Xavier, Peace, Love & Joy Mentor, CA

The work that I have done with The Diamond Co-Creative System® has been truly transformational for me. Learning how to use the Diamond Co-Creation Codes and Elevation Codes have helped me to transform my physical, mental, emotional, spiritual, and financial life. I have studied and practiced many different systems, but I have never been able to achieve the kind of results that I have created with this powerful System and its Codes.

What I love about the System is that it's practical, giving me grounded results, yet incorporates Universal spiritual principles with very simple and clear instructions for me to co-create a life I want to live. And, it has opened a pathway to fulfill my Soul's purpose in my business and become even more joyous and prosperous as I contribute to others and the world.

– Diana Concoff Morgan, Digital Impact Strategist, CA

I began working with The Diamond Co-Creative System® and its Codes in 2020, when I realized I had to be a vibrational match to what I wanted to bring into my life. I began to focus twice a day on working with the System. And, at 75 years old, I am now enjoying an amazing romantic relationship with a man who is my energetic match, and more money is coming into my life as well. The System works!!!

The System has turned my life upside down in the most wonderful ways including healing old family wounds and dynamics, creating confidence and trust in myself, and starting a new business in which I'm passionate about and love to serve others. The Codes are more and more a part of who I am … it's so very powerful!

– Cynthia Hollins, Grief Coach & Spiritual Energy Healer, CA

Contents

ACKNOWLEDGMENTS

I want to thank and acknowledge both my etheric and earth teams who have helped bring this work forward. Foremost, none of this would be possible without the Divine and my Soul guiding me; my heart is filled with gratitude for this opportunity to be of service that the Divine gave me. I am so grateful for the etheric Guides and Councils who I co-create with and the wisdom that they share. I especially want to thank Archangel Michael, Metatron, St. Germaine, Lord Melchizedek, and the Council of ALL who assisted in bringing forth The Diamond Co-Creative System® and its body of work. They have always been there to inspire, guide, and support me along the way.

Thank you to my family and friends who have loved and supported me throughout my own personal journey and the development and evolution of The Diamond Co-Creative System®. To my mom, Tillie and stepdad, David Nelson who stood by me even when they did not understand or approve of what I was doing. To my brother, David Butler, who I can always count on. To my Aunt CC who was my biggest cheerleader as I grew up and kept reminding me to believe in myself and reassured me that I can do it.

My eternal gratitude goes to my friend, Diana Concoff Morgan, who has been by my side rooting me on and there to bounce ideas off of when needed. To Marge Bruce, who has been there for the last twenty years sharing continuous friendship and support. To James Hughes who put me on this path of energetic healing and always insisted I would be a healer and teacher even when I denied it. To Stephen Brennan who has witnessed my own evolution since 2005 and supported me along the way with his guidance and wisdom. And, to Karen Renee Halseth for the healing and transformation that she has provided to me, personally and professionally.

My appreciation goes to several who have assisted in the evolution of Co-Create Your Success and The Diamond Co-Creative System® over the years: to Meryt for the original art renderings of the Diamond Co-Creation Codes, to Terrie MacNicol in her assistance with updates to the Universal 'L' and other graphics, to Jim Vujovich and Aaron Pyne for updating the Diamond Co-Creation Codes, to Melissa Miller for the branding, to Mariah Lander and Tess Sawyer for graphics and assistance with updates of The Diamond Co-Creative System®, and to Andy Drake assisting me with other graphics and website development.

Thank you to our awesome SOUL (Serving Others within Unified Love) team within Co-Create Your Success who are always assisting in different ways so that the System continues to make a positive impact in the world. These include Linda Rielly who has been a staunch supporter of me and the System and Taylor Matzelle, my virtual assistant, who makes my life so much easier with her contributions. And, to Maurine Xavier, an accredited Diamond Co-Creative System® practitioner, coach, and teacher who has taken on the System as an integral part of her practice and makes a difference in people's lives with it.

My thanks go to my editor, Catharine Bramkamp who held my hand along the way of writing a book and for your gentle guidance that made it seem possible. I am grateful for Pam Murphy and Michelle VanGeest in bringing this book home and getting it published in a masterful way.

And, finally, to my clients along the way who have embraced The Diamond Co-Creative System® as a modality that changed their lives. During the journey with my clients, I found what works best for the healing, transformation, and evolution process as well as ways to create and manifest with the System, so it became a practical tool with real-life results of Love, joy, peace, trust, and abundant prosperity. Thank you for being willing to change and to evolve into your ALL!

PROLOGUE

I am so grateful for my life. I am passionate about my work and those that I attract to being in the Diamond Co-Creator community. During my own journey, I learned to Truly believe in and trust myself and all the guidance I receive from the Divine, my Spirit Guides and the Councils, and the Universe.

I began Co-Create Your Success in 2001 with the mission to spread the consciousness and vibration of Love to others through healing the past, enlivening the spirit, and empowering the True Self. This hasn't changed since then but it has evolved into upgrading into 5th Dimension consciousness and a new way of BE-ing.

Even before people were talking about the shifts that were occurring from the 3rd to the 5th Dimension, I was writing articles and teaching courses in 2006 about operating, creating, and living in the 5th Dimension. Personally, I was going through these shifts and experienced 5th Dimension Principles, vibrations, and ways of living that were being channeled in from my Spirit Guides and the Divine.

This is the shifts from fear to Love, from survival to thrival, and from scarcity into abundance. It is about letting go of the past so you can be present in the moment and live in the now.

This is about moving from the 3rd Dimension paradigm into 5th Dimension vibrations and ways of BE-ing. I have had my own journey in making these shifts changing my life, relationships, and business from pain, suffering, and struggling to this life I always wanted.

I invite you to allow us (me and my etheric team of Spirit Guides and the Council of ALL) to be of service so you too can create and live the life you have always wanted. If you allow yourself to receive the many lessons, the Principles & Codes, and the power they offer to work for you, within you, and through you, then all aspects of your life can improve and upgrade into your ALL.

With The Diamond Co-Creative System®, your life, relationships, health and well-being, spirituality, finances, and career or business will never be the same. You will enter the stratosphere of Infinite Possibilities and SOUL-utions beyond your imagination. It will stretch you, take you, and deliver you into the unknown and into your fullest potential of the ALL!

Let me share a bit about my journey …

It was 1986. When people met me (and even my friends and family), they saw an attractive, powerful, tenacious, and successful woman. I was doing all the 'right' things and accomplishing what I (and they) thought I 'should' do.

From the outside, my life looked great. But on the inside, it was quite a different story. Inside, I was a scared, wounded little girl shaking in my boots, worried that someone would find out who I really was and what was really going on within me. I felt like 'at the effect' of life instead of being 'at the cause' of it.

I had to be perfect ... the perfect daughter, the perfect wife, the perfect friend, and the perfect employee. I had to keep my mask on, so they wouldn't know the truth. I felt like a fraud, fooling everyone around me, including myself. I felt like a broken-down woman, trapped in a marriage that wasn't working, and with little or no Self-esteem or Self-respect.

I looked everywhere to feel better ... for other's approval, acceptance, and Love. I suffered from emotional eating to stuff my feelings, and excessive shopping to try to fill the holes I felt within. I could drop $3000-$5000 in two hours at Nordstrom but still feel like I didn't have enough, or that I was enough. The fear and uneasiness that churned in the pit of my stomach never went away.

I was afraid to feel it. What would happen if I felt it ... would I melt away in the vastness of my tears and fears? I felt numb and operated on automatic pilot. I would create crises or drama in my life, my relationships, my finances, or at my job just to feel alive in some way, even if it was destructive. My ex-husband and I would create fights since we did not know how to communicate constructively, or to be open and vulnerable, or to let Love in on any level. We would escalate the fights to just feel something and hopefully to connect with one another.

I was so disconnected from me, from others, and from my feelings, my worth, my faith, my desires, my passion, and my creativity. Here I was 30 years old, feeling like I was 90, with no spark or energy left within me.

I would sit in the middle of a church service with streams of tears running down my face. They were not tears of joy, but tears of sadness, anguish, and despair. I envied the others at the service ... they looked alive, joyous, and loving; they looked like the spirit of the Divine was in their lives.

I wanted what they had. To feel connected. To be inspired. To Love me, to Love life, and to Love Divine Source once again. To feel the spirit and Love of the Angels (both etheric Spiritual Guides and earth Angels like my Aunt CC). The pain and inner struggle were so great and in my face that I quit going to church.

I went through three years of intense psychotherapy (individual, marriage, and group each week!), but nothing really shifted. It helped me become aware of my problems and their source, but it did not heal or resolve them. Eventually, I divorced my husband because I realized he was another way I was trying to fill myself up and the relationship was steeped in co-dependency that was trying to mend a deeply wounded heart.

I read the book, *Co-Dependent No More* by Melody Beadie and thought, *how was I ever going to heal?* I felt like I was the worst person ever and had no hope of it changing. I felt I was deep in a hole without a ladder to climb out of it. It was so daunting.

Only when I discovered energetic healing and the results that were created did my life finally begin to shift. This started my true healing journey. It helped me heal at the very core of my pain and issues, and the way I thought, felt, believed, and lived life began to change. It revitalized my own spirit within and created a connection to my Soul's Essence and to the Divine.

This is what led me to my mission because I had to learn how to live and BE. I needed to love myself first before I could truly love others and be able to make the contribution I am here to make.

And so, the *awareness* of my Soul's journey began…

CHAPTER ONE

My Soul Got Me Fired!

My Soul got me fired.

At forty years old, I lived in Florida, in a beautiful custom-built home I designed myself, and worked in my dream job as a Vice President of Marketing and Sales for a publishing firm. Then the call came, "The Tampa office is being shut down and we want you to transfer to New York."

Ten years earlier, I would've jumped at the chance to live in Manhattan. I loved my job. I'd successfully climbed the corporate ladder in a male-dominated company to the position of Vice President managing a staff of fourteen. I worked seventy hours a week and traveled around the country. I was doing everything I thought I 'should' do to be successful.

And yet, was I happy? Not really. I had no personal life. I hadn't attracted the love I wanted. I just worked, checking off all of the 'should' boxes of my career. So, of course, even though I wanted to say no to the transfer to New York, I said yes.

I didn't feel empowered to say no because I had no idea what else I'd do. I was in serious debt, needed the paycheck, and didn't believe in myself or trust I could choose something different. The 'shoulds' ruled me.

And my worries, doubts, shame, confusion, and fears ran me:

What if I'm not enough or good enough?

To make it I must work hard, sacrifice, and do, do, do.

I have to prove I'm lovable, worthy, and deserving of all that I want.

The truth was, I really had no clue what I wanted. I was so lost and could no longer feel or even name my passions. On automatic pilot, I just put one foot in front of the other without really considering the path I was going down. So, when the powers that be made their unilateral decision to close the Tampa office without consulting me, and to keep my job, I begrudgingly said yes and went along with moving to New York.

On January 2, 1997, my first day in Manhattan, a strange dream startled me awake. I shook it off and went into the office at 7 a.m. to set-up and get started.

I was the good little soldier who put on the "I got this!" game face. I willed myself to make this work. I began visiting different departments to check on projects. With each check-in, I became increasingly upset. My General Manager had undermined everything I implemented without consulting me *again* before making changes.

At 11 a.m., we had our weekly phone call. As we began the call, something came over me. I felt a surge of energy flowing through me from the top of my head all the way down my body and taking over what I was saying.

It wasn't me who was saying the words. It was my Soul talking, and said, "Why are you changing everything I implemented and not talking with me before you do it? I work long and hard for this company and it seems like you don't value my expertise and what I bring to the table. It's so frustrating!"

I took a deep breath and paused to consider what I was saying. But I couldn't stop it and continued to say, "And why are there executive meetings that I'm not being invited to? This is exactly how you treated Gary, edging him out, giving him all the responsibility but no authority to do what he thought was best. When I accepted this position, you and I had agreement that this is *not* how you would treat me, and I would *not* be your puppet. This is *not* what I signed up for. Why in the hell are you moving me to New York when you don't respect me and what I offer and do?"

It was like a cartoon. As the words tumbled out, I tried to gather them and literally stuff them back in my mouth. Interestingly, I'd stuffed my feelings for eons, so this was nothing new.

It felt like there was another Amanda in the room. This remarkable surge of energy pulsating through me felt amazing … it was so empowering. Knowing what I know now, it was my Soul taking over and letting me know, "Enough is enough. You're done here and it's time to move on."

When I hung up the phone, I thought, *Well, as a marketer, this is not the way to convince my boss to let me keep my job — I just nailed my coffin shut.* Two hours later, I was called into the CFO's office and fired.

As I walked out of his office, I felt immediate relief like a huge weight was lifted off my shoulders. I thought, *My Soul just got me fired! It has set me free. Thank you!*

I remembered my earlier dream. Its message assured me: *Everything will be okay. It may be rough for a while, but you will emerge with the sun shining brightly upon you.* At the time, I had no idea what it meant, but for some reason, I trusted it.

I had no plan B and really didn't know what I wanted for myself. I was well-respected in the industry, so I had many potential opportunities. However, after interviewing for any new marketing job, I left the interviews feeling completely drained. I would sit in the parking lots crying and feeling defeated. I had no spark or enthusiasm to continue on with this career path. I knew something had to change, and a new marketing job was not the answer.

I felt immense anger and tumbled into deep depression. Two months later, I literally fell to my knees in utter despair and asked God for help. And truth be told, I really didn't ask. I *told* God that if things didn't change in six months, I'd be out of here (yes, suicide). I yelled out in hopelessness, sobbing, and hands raised to the Heavens, "God, I'm willing to do anything that will help me and my life to change — just show me the way."

Well, what I didn't know is when I did this, I was asking to be put on a 'fast track' of healing, transformation, and expansion. I'd been on a spiritual path for years and recently learned about energetic healing and its power to help me heal. This was the path, and it was now time to get serious about my healing.

I attended workshops, not understanding energetics at all, what Chakras were and how they affected you and your Energy Bodies, but I knew in my heart that I was in the 'right' place. I had no idea what I was doing, but what I *did* know I always felt better after an energetic healing session.

Getting fired and exploring something unknown was the catalyst and opportunity for my Soul to take over and show me the way. I had felt dead inside for years, so I knew things had to change within and around me if I wanted to live a fulfilling and happy life.

When I started with energetic healing, I became alive again. I felt energy moving within me. My feelings started surfacing, and this time I began to recognize when something was 'off' for me. I resisted at first, because I feared if I opened the gates to my feelings, I would drown in a flood of emotions and dissolve into nothingness. And, for a time, I did.

But by dissolving the past and the 'shoulds,' the walls around my heart began to drop. The old thoughts, beliefs, and feelings about who I thought I was and what I should do began to shift. I learned should is really a four-letter word because when we 'should' upon ourselves, we bring our-selves down–it's tied to fear, judgment, and perfectionism.

I was able to let go and tap into the REAL me …

REAL …
Realized Energy Aligned with Love

Did this happen overnight? Not by a long shot.

But my process began to accelerate in 2001 when I channeled in The Diamond Co-Creative System® (the System) with its Diamond Co-Cre-ation Codes and techniques. With this System, I discovered how to shift fear and denseness, and move past energetics such as pain, suffering, and struggle, and turn them into Love and the flow of peace, ease, and grace.

Within this book, my Spirit Guides and the Council of ALL share with you their profound wisdom, teachings, and support. Much of it was chan-neled from the Guides and Councils, as well as what I have learned along the way in my own quest for healing, transformation, and expansion into my ALL … Abundant Light and Love of me and what I am here to do.

CHAPTER TWO

You Are Energy &
Your Energetic Integrity

Everything is energy, including you. Your thoughts, beliefs, feelings, words, and actions are all energy and propel your vibrational frequencies out into the world.

If your energy is positive, then you're adding to the Light and Higher frequencies within yourself and to those around you. If negative, you are simply adding to the fear, denseness, and lower frequencies within life.

The more you can stay present in the moment, the quicker you can raise your frequencies and sustain a life within 5th Dimension vibrations, which in turn will aid you to easily navigate your journey through the challenging times of life and the world. It is always a Conscious Choice to remain where you are at, or to choose differently if it doesn't work for you or no longer serves you.

Let's talk about your cellular memory and energetic make-up. You, as a Soul, are a unique set of adamantine particles which are the most minute form of energy in the Universe. Your adamantine particles not only retain all experiences but influence your interpretation of those experiences, conditioning, and programming. If you've deemed an experience as positive, then your adamantine particles are aligned with the Sacred Geometry of your Divine blueprint of Love.

However, if you've interpreted the experience as negative in some way, it becomes 'wired up' as a negative vibration and becomes your 'story.' Negative experiences will skew the adamantine particles and create an out of alignment with your original Divine blueprint of Love. The result is an incomplete energetic cycle which forms a pattern and a 'wiring' within your neuropathways that will need to be healed and completed if you want different results.

Your neuropathways are created through your patterns of thoughts, beliefs, and feelings which lead to your behaviors, habits, and actions, thus your results. Physics and science have proven that when patterns gather and repeat themselves, they reveal both their interconnection and neuroscience pathways which form into physical matter and manifestations.

The only way to shift a negative pattern is to disrupt the pattern, which then can create new neuropathways. You must first release and complete the past energetic cycle, then re-pattern it to create a new cellular 'wiring,' thus a new neuropathway. The Diamond Co-Creative System® and its Diamond Co-Creation Codes (the Codes) help you to do this and actually accelerate your process to realign and recalibrate your energetics.

The Codes assist in realigning the adamantine particles back to your original Divine blueprint of Love at a cellular level, and this is why it works! This is how the past, patterns, issues, and old paradigms can be resolved completely and *once and for all.*

Your Soul is the Mastery of who you Truly are–your True Nature–Love. It holds all your gifts, talents, and the wisdom that you have gained from every lifetime. It does not hold the pain, or any unresolved issues from the past. It does not hold any out of alignment energies to that of Love. Those experiences and energies are held in your Akashic records, and in your cellular memory. It is what you came here to heal and complete.

When people talk about the "Dark Night of the Soul," they really mean the "Dark Night of the Egoic Self/Mind." It is your Egoic Self that's going through the pain, suffering, and struggle of the shift, which is being called forth, not your Soul. Your Soul is full of pristine Light and your Divinity which is that of Love.

In order for your Soul's energies to embody within you, you have to clear the decks, so to speak. This is why you are called to be on a healing and transformation journey. It's important to clear the old energetics: thoughts, beliefs, feelings, imprints, encodings, vows, agreements, patterns, and paradigms from this lifetime, and others that no longer serve or work for you.

But now the game is changing. You are now entering a time of accelerated expansion to assist with your evolution and ascension. The focus now is–what is my MORE … Moving Onward Respecting Eternity?

MORE ...
Moving Onward Respecting Eternity

You are an Eternal Spiritual Being who is living life on this planet in a Physical Body. Eternity is the Infinite ... Infinite Universal energies and expansions, Infinite Love, Infinite Possibilities, and Infinite SOUL-utions.

And now, your Physical Body also yearns for an upgrade. It yearns for evolution to become more of a 'Light' Body and your Soul is more than happy to assist you in doing so! Your mission, if you so choose to accept it, is to clear the pathway for your Soul's energies to enter into Physical Body as you heal the denseness held within it.

Therefore, you have been called to be so diligent with your Energetic and Emotional Integrity and to heal the past. And, by doing so, this leads you to a deeper sense of Emotional and Spiritual maturity, which is also part of your Soul's evolution, so you can embody your ALL ... Abundant (Absolute) Light & Love.

ALL ...
Abundant (Absolute) Light & Love

By being aware and conscious of how you are energetically feeling, you can create Energetic and Emotional Integrity. This helps you to notice what you are thinking, feeling, believing, saying, and doing.

And, if you need to do some emotional release and healing work due to a trigger of some sort, you can choose to address it. As you become aware of whether your frequency is low due to the type of energy you are focusing upon, or might be affected due to what (or who) may have come into your energy fields, then you can Consciously Choose to pivot into a Higher frequency and be in your own Energetic and Emotional Integrity.

Knowing what 'normal' is for you is key to maintaining your Energetic and Emotional Integrity. When you don't 'feel' like yourself, it can often be accompanied by physical symptoms, such as a headache or backache, a cough or sore throat, or body aches or tiredness, for example. Or maybe you suddenly feel depleted, drained or stressed, yet you haven't done anything out of the ordinary to cause it. This is important information for you to get to the bottom of what happened to energetically derail you.

In addition, Emotional Integrity means you do your own work, and you don't project your unresolved emotions upon another. You take responsibility for how you feel and energetically complete what no longer serves you.

As you raise your vibrations, you are actually developing a 'new normal' … a new rhythm, a new way of BE-ing, and a new commitment of Self-care within your Energetic and Emotional Integrity. You allow yourself the space to develop this and listen within. By doing so, this allows for the Soul's Essence to emBODY even more.

As you become better and better in doing this, you will recognize when you are playing, creating, and living within a 3rd Dimension paradigm of lower frequencies that will manifest the same results. But if you're playing, creating, and living in the Higher frequencies of the 5th Dimension, you will be in your natural state of BE-ing which is Love and create different outcomes.

CHAPTER THREE

Shifting From the 3rd Dimension to the 5th & Why It Matters

Humankind has entered a Shift of the Ages and it's accelerating our ascension process. This is evident by all the chaos, uncertainty, and upheavals occurring in our world, and for many, in their lives. We are shifting from the 3rd Dimension to the 5th Dimension which is essential to help humanity move in Love and Unity consciousness.

'Ascend' means filling your cells with Light, which transforms the denseness of your Physical Body and allows you to embody your Soul's Essence. The result is the creation of your 'Light' Body within your Physical Body, which contributes to your ascension and continual evolution.

Your ascension process is a journey, not a destination. It's important to know you can now choose to fully embody the metaphysical and spiritual changes that are taking place within and around you. You do not need to leave the planet to ascend; you have the opportunity to do it now within the physical on this earth.

When you do, you will have the opportunity to step into the Love that you Truly are, to help humanity in the ways you are guided, and to be a steward of this beautiful planet in which we live upon. You are here for a reason and to make a difference, no matter how small or how grand.

We each have a choice to make. We can choose to evolve as individuals and allow our Souls to guide us into the Higher frequencies of the 5th Dimension. The more your energetic vibration is in High frequency, the more you attract High frequency people, opportunities, and possibilities into your life. This is very important, because you *always*, and *in all ways*, are attracting matching energies and you magnetize what you focus upon.

The 3rd Dimension

The 3rd Dimension is a denser frequency hallmarked by fear, separation, duality (either/or, good/bad, and right/wrong), me vs. we thinking and behaviors, competition, power and control over others, wars, and greed. You are a reactor versus being in a neutral place of response. You are driven by ambition and achievements, rather than meaning and contribution.

The 3rd Dimension keeps you stuck in a linear timeline where the past continues to be dragged into the present to influence your current reality and to affect your future. It is a timeline that creates the same old results by recycling all of the old issues … Physically, Emotionally, Mentally, and Spiritually. It prevents you from being fully present in the moment and stepping into the future that you want to create, which is your Divine birthright.

The Emotional Energy Body stores your feelings, and your emotions … *energy in motion* which are the gauges as to what is going on within you. They reveal energetic patterns which are either 'in' or 'out' of alignment with Love.

When your energy *is not* aligned, it will fuel your fears and negative feelings such as not feeling worthy, deserving, not enough or good enough, and disempowered. When your energetic pattern *is* aligned with Love, your feelings are amplified in positive ways energized through vibrations of Love, joy, acceptance, compassion, peace, passion, ease, and grace.

The Mental Energy Body creates your thoughts, beliefs, and perceptions. In the 3rd Dimension, the Mental Body is run by the egoic mind which believes it's in control and only it knows how to protect you to keep you safe and secure. It doesn't like the unknown, so it will stay with what's familiar, even if it's uncomfortable.

The egoic mind lives mostly in illusion, separation, and with skewed perceptions, while operating from fear, survival — fight, flight, or freeze mode, and the past. It is attached to how the results 'should' show up and what they 'should' be. The egoic mind doesn't like to let go or even forgive until you make a Conscious Choice to shift it.

The Conscious Choice is to lift the egoic mind up into your Divine Mind guided by your Soul's Essence and the Divine. Your Divine Mind shifts the energetics of the Mental Energy Body into 5th Dimensional frequencies and opens into the flow and acceptance of Divine Timing and Divine Unfoldment. This leads you to your Soul-aligned Possibilities and SOUL-utions, which directs you into manifesting what's in your Highest Order and Infinite Diamond Potential.

Sometimes, your thoughts, beliefs, and perceptions are run by your emotions. If you are in a negative vibration, whether through your feelings, thoughts, beliefs, or perceptions, they continue to play out the karmic game ... *cause and effect*. It keeps you in a low energetic pattern and cycle which never seems to end, until you choose to energetically complete it.

As you begin 'lightening' up (ascending), by releasing patterns of old programming, conditioning, and imprints, your vibrational frequency rises. You move from the 3rd Dimension to stabilize within the 4th Dimension.

The 4th Dimension

The 4th Dimension is the energetic bridge between the 3rd and 5th Dimensions. In the 4th Dimension, there's a glimpse of the Divine; you begin to question your perceived state of reality. You realize there is a spiritual aspect to you and life and that there's much more going on than your Physical Body and physical matter. You begin to explore spirituality and spiritual practices when you embark into a 4th Dimension paradigm.

You venture into the unknown and the egoic mind is shaken up; it tries to hold on to what it knows but the doorway has been opened for the more of you ... your Soul and the Divine to engage with you. You begin to understand that it takes more energy to keep you in a state of fear and separation, rather than to let go, do the 'work,' and allow Love, Light, and Spirit into your life.

You become the observer and start to determine what works for you and what doesn't, what you like and what you don't. You determine what you need and want and give yourself permission to ask for it. You begin to think and feel differently, which shifts your beliefs, perceptions, and patterns; what was 'normal' for you isn't anymore and you begin to discover a 'new' you which allows for Soul alignment and embodiment.

This assists you to transform your negative, low frequency conscious-ness into a more positive vibration state of BE-ing. As you shift into the 4th Dimension on a more consistent basis, you begin to trust there's a different way of living life and the egoic mind lets go of its hold on you little by little. It no longer runs the show; it happens by becoming more aware and conscious of what is going on within and around you.

Once you have stabilized in the 4th, you then move into the elevated vibrations of 5th Dimension living. You are ready to experience more and more expansion by living in the now within Love and Unity consciousness which recognizes we are all One Global family.

The 5th Dimension

Within the 5th Dimension, you are a Soul-aligned creator and genera-tor of your own life. You think, feel, believe, say, and do in a Soul-aligned manner. You believe you have the power within you to shift your life, your outcomes, or any circumstance even when it's difficult.

As you operate and create within the 5th Dimension, you become aware of yourself as a Master Creator and Co-Creator, and a multi-dimen-sional Divine being. You are spiritually oriented and bring continuous spiritual practices and ways of BE-ing into your life. You're connected to your Soul's Essence, Divine Source, and the Universe, and you ask for their assistance to guide and support you.

The 5th Dimension promotes Oneness and Unity consciousness, where co-creation, collaboration, and cooperation with the Divine and with others for the 'Highest Good of All' is a priority. It is the sharing of resources and wealth, and where there is reverence for all Beings. It is where inclusivity accepts and honors diversity. You realize that we are all interconnected so it's important how we accept and treat one another.

In the 5th Dimension, the only timeline is the present moment. Living in the now … not dragging in the past or fussing about the future. It is where you Consciously Choose LOVE … Living Only (One) Vibrant Energy.

LOVE …
Living Only (One) Vibrant Energy

Within the 5th Dimension is a state of BE-ing where synchronic-ity is constant and you recognize the 'coincidences,' messages, and opportunities that come your way. It is where the magic and alchemy of manifestation seems to happen easily and quickly through Love, joy, grace, passion, faith, trust, and belief, even amid challenges.

Here is a chart to help you in becoming aware of and recognizing what frequency you're vibing within; it provides you a roadmap of the shifts within your energetics and consciousness from the 3rd Dimension to the 4th to the 5th Dimension:

What Dimension & Energetics Do You Operate, Create & Live Within?

3rd Dimension (3D) Ambition/Reactor	4th Dimension (4D) The Bridge – Meaning/Observer	5th Dimension (5D) Soul-Aligned/Creator & Generator
Oriented in Masculine Energies Typically Wounded & Stuck in the Past; Learn through Pain, Suffering & Struggle	**Bringing in Feminine Energies** Allow to Receive & Claim Your Power; Connect with Divine Source & the Universe; become more Spiritually attuned & know there is MORE!	**Unified Field & Union Within** Create Sacred Union within all aspects of you … Masculine, Feminine, Inner Child, Soul & the Divine; Learn through Joy; Move into ALL … Absolute Light & Love
Ego-Driven	Heart-Centered	Soul-urged & Soul-full
Fear-Based	Love-Based	Divine/Soul-inspired & Highly Intuitive
Creates & Wears Masks	Focuses on Identification & Roles	Soul Embodiment & Soul's Expression through your Personality & Egoic Self
Survival	A Dance Between Surviving & Thriving	Thrive & Love - Living Only Vibrant Energy
'Either/Or'	Embracing the 'AND'	Live the 'AND'

3rd Dimension (3D) Ambition/Reactor	4th Dimension (4D) The Bridge — Meaning/Observer	5th Dimension (5D) Soul-Aligned/Creator & Generator
Separation & Exclusion	Togetherness	Inclusion & Unification
Co-Dependency	De-Entanglement & Seeker	Inter-Dependency & Co-Creator
Competition & Lose/Lose	Try to Cooperate & Usually Win/Lose	Collaboration, Co-Creation & Win/Win
Lack & Scarcity	Just Enough or Enough	Plenty & Prosperity Consciousness
Doubt, Worry & Anxiety	Faith, Trust & Belief	Knows the Universe Advocates for You
'Shoulds'	Purpose	True Satisfaction & Fulfillment
Judgmental & Critical	Less Negative Self-Talk & Acceptance	Compassion & Authenticity
Pain & Struggle	Healing & Transformation	Expansion & Evolution
Chase	Convince or Enroll	Magnetize & Steward
Needs to Get Energy	Reciprocity	Generosity & Contributor
Push Against	Push/Pull Energy	Allowance & in Divine Flow
Force	Strength	Stand in Your Divine Power & Authority
Seeks Fame	Needs to be Important & Recognized	Influencer & Positive Impact
Restrictive	More Open to Receive & Open-Minded	Infinite Possibilities & SOUL-utions
Entitled; Someone Owes You	More Honor, Respect & Thankfulness	In Grace & Gratitude for All
Confusion & Lacks Clarity	Conscious Choice & Decisions	Soul-aligned with Divine Wisdom
Inertia and/or Overwhelm	Conscious Actions	Soul-driven Creation & Manifestation

Know that even if you attain and sustain a 5th Dimension frequency, you may occasionally dip back into the 3rd or 4th Dimensions. But here is the good news, you can *always* choose differently. And, when you operate, create, and live in the 5th Dimension, you can navigate through challenging times in ease and grace with SOUL-utions you might not have even thought of or considered.

Now, how do you ideally shift your vibrations more quickly and easily? There is no need to excavate and continually drudge up the past. It only requires a commitment and willingness to release and complete the past, so it does not continue to be your 'story' with the same results.

The radical SOUL-ution to do so is utilizing The Diamond Co-Creative System® as you do your work–your healing, transformation, and evolution into the ALL of who you are and what you do.

CHAPTER FOUR

The SOUL-ution ...
The Diamond Co-Creative System®

In 2001, I was preparing to lead a group to swim with the dolphins in Bimini, a Bahama out-island. Two days before leaving, I 'downloaded' a set of symbols. I was told that this is the first time the symbols had been back on the planet since Atlantis.

I was given clear instructions as to what to do with them as I traveled to Bimini. Bimini is where some of the ancient lands of Atlantis have been discovered, so this was very serendipitous. I was told by my Spirit Guides not to show them to anyone until a ceremony occurred while I was in Bimini. As a newbie to channeling (in this lifetime), I did what I was told and trusted there was a reason for it.

It turned out this ceremony was in the waters; it included "seven sisters" who were on the trip, the dolphins, and Galactic participation. The ceremony was done to activate the symbols which we now call the Diamond Co-Creation Codes, and they collaborate with one another as a System.

The ceremony was done to protect them from ever being used for ill will or to harm anyone who uses them personally, or with others. It also infused them with their Divine-cell consciousness to help all of us on earth reach our Highest Order and fullest Infinite Diamond Potential.

Later, I learned that I initially developed this System as a scientist back in Atlantis. In that past life, I was dedicated to understanding energy and how to work with energy so it could assist the evolution of humankind and the earth.

It was time for this energy to come back during this lifetime to help with the shifts that are occurring within humanity and on the planet through the ascension process of moving from the 3rd Dimension to the 5th Dimension. And, to assist in elevating the vibrations and consciousness of humankind to Oneness and Unification so that "the Good of All" is prevalent in All things and All peoples.

But at the time, I had no idea what the symbols were or what they did. I was guided that I would use them for myself first, then teach others.

Now, understand when I was guided back then, I usually went *kicking and screaming all the way*. I eventually acquiesced because I knew what I had done in the past didn't work, so I was willing to try anything new.

However, I wasn't always a willing participant. Many times, I argued with the Divine, my Guides, and my Soul as to what I was being asked to do. My egoic mind liked to be in control and wanted to know the who, what, when, how, and why, since this guidance thing was an unknown. My egoic mind liked things just the way they were; it avoided the unknown, even though I was unhappy and unfulfilled. It liked the familiar, even if the familiar was growing more and more uncomfortable and no longer served me.

This usually manifested in my inability to listen to my intuition or guidance; my egoic mind thought it knew better. It also meant playing it safe, and not rocking the boat (especially with family and friends) … that would be scary to be considered weird and not have people like me or what I was doing.

BUT my Soul was done with that! It reached out to my egoic mind and personality Self to ask me to co-create a new life and a new way of BE-ing together. Over time, I learned how to trust my intuition, my Soul, and the guidance shared with me. I learned to trust and believe in myself and the Creator within me.

The Diamond Co-Creative System® *became my SOUL-ution to thrive and prosper …*

About The Diamond Co-Creative System®

The Diamond Co-Creative System® (the System) is a leading-edge alchemical 12th Dimensional technology derived from Sacred Geometry. The 12th Dimension holds Unity consciousness and the High frequencies of Oneness leading you to live and create within the 5th Dimension vibrations of Love, joy, flow, co-creation, and abundant prosperity.

Sacred Geometry is the science and vibrational energetic blueprint for all creation. It is formed through the vibrations of Love, which is also the harmonic configuration of your Soul's Divine blueprint and the construct of the Universe.

As a human being, *you* are composed of Sacred Geometry within your physical structure, cells, and cellular memory. Sacred geometry bridges science and spirituality by bringing spirit and nature together in all life forms. It is the foundation of all that exists and materializes in physical form.

Metatron's Cube

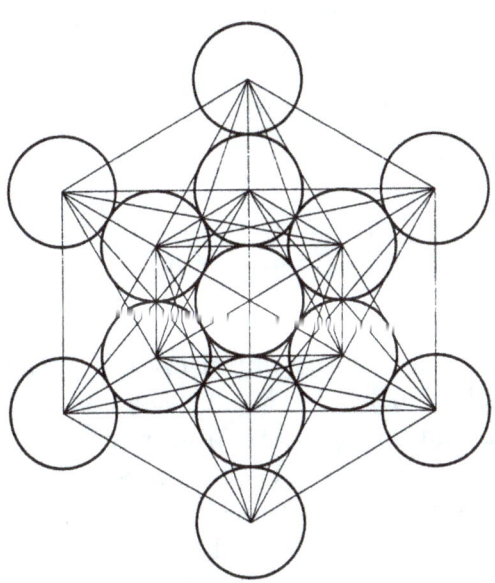

Metatron's Cube contains all the Sacred Geometric shapes and science of the Divine's creation and represents the patterns of the Universe's construct. The complex structure of Metatron's Cube derives from the ancient configuration of the Flower of Life, which holds the vibrations of Divine Love and language of Light.

Love is the energy and blueprint within the Universe that connects all things. It is considered a strong energy conductor, capable of transcending negative low-frequency energy and attracting positive energies, which tap into Higher frequencies and the Infinite. Love provides a pathway to connect and co-create within the Infinite quantum field of the Universe.

The Diamond Co-Creation Codes

Initially in 2001, there were nine Universal Diamond Co-Creation Codes with an additional four Galactic Diamond Co-Creation Codes that were downloaded during 2015. All thirteen Diamond Co-Creation Codes (Codes) are each designed upon the Sacred Geometry of Metatron's Cube along with different Universal Light language, symbols, and sound frequencies. This gives each Code its unique and specific energetic qualities. The Codes work within the science *and* the spiritual aspect of the Universe.

Each Code has a specific name, purpose, and vibrational qualities that enhance your work with your Chakras and Energy Bodies, which in turn aid in healing and transforming the energetics of the past–this lifetime and others, imprints, encodings, conditioning, and programming. With these Codes you can realign and repattern your energetics and bring you back into the present time thus your past won't dictate your results or the future.

The Codes will move into areas such as your Chakras and Energy Bodies which need assistance at whatever level you require. They each hold a Divine-cell consciousness and purpose, so they know what you need and want (even if you don't, especially at a subconscious level). The System will only help create what's in your Highest order and Infinite Diamond Potential.

The System goes to the core origination point and the cellular memory for healing. Unlike other modalities, which may *only* address the symptoms of issues and past pain, the System helps heal and transform from the origination–this lifetime's experiences, past lives, family imprints, or lineage and genetic encodings. With the System, you can experience immediate and sustainable healings, transformations, and expansions!

Plus, the Codes go beyond healing to assist you to manifest and evolve into fulfilling your Soul's purpose and plan. And, to create the life, relationships, health and well-being, wealth, and career or business that you Truly want and were meant to live.

The Codes do not compete with any other modality or spiritual practice. They will only enhance them from the 12th Dimension where "All is One."

What's cool is that you don't need to understand how it works. Only *believe* that it does. It's not necessary to intellectually understand how the Codes work for the Codes to help you.

This is because this lifetime is about *feeling,* not about thinking your way through life. If the egoic mind tries to figure out how and why the Codes work, it will get in the way of what you want and need. It doesn't have to be hard or a struggle for you to heal, transform, manifest, expand, and evolve.

There's no right or wrong way of using the Codes; you can't do it wrong. There's no need to be perfect in using the System. You will learn and experience different ways of utilizing it as you use it more. The System helps you build trust and confidence in your own intuition and guidance as well as opening your Clair gifts such as claircognizant, clairsentience, clairaudience, and clairvoyance.

If you're empathetic, the Codes will help you develop a sense and understanding of your energy, other's energy, or even the collective's energy. The System will help you to be more discerning and to create your own Energetic and Emotional Integrity. It accelerates your Soul's journey and evolution as it helps you heal, transform, align, and manifest what's in your Highest Order and Infinite Diamond Potential.

The System is the SOUL-ution that I was looking for but didn't know it at the time.

When the System was downloaded to me, I rejected it, questioned it, and resisted it. Even though it was the answer to my prayers to change my life, on a subconscious level I liked being in crisis, chaos, drama, victim-hood, and confusion. It was what I knew … to be reactive and to be in survival mode.

It gave my egoic mind something to do — I would create a problem then my ego was ready to step in and fix it. My egoic mind felt its job was to keep me safe, secure, and protected at any cost, including sacrific-ing my happiness and dreams. Venturing into the unknown was at best, uncomfortable, at worst, scary.

What was the discomfort? Not knowing what I desired or even liked anymore. I chased after answers. I had an insatiable *need* to find my pas-sion and purpose — what was the reason for me being here? I was having financial difficulties and health challenges, too. I was confused and stuck in trying to see any way out of my circumstances.

All of this was the result of living by my 'shoulds.' These came from what I learned and observed in my family and from society, as well as through old 3rd Dimensional conditioning and programming. I was super co-dependent and wanted everyone to like me, so I could fit in. I looked for love, acceptance, and validation from the outside to feel safe and secure rather than from within. I had huge abandonment, rejection, and victim issues 'running' the show.

I intellectually understood what I believed was wrong with me but never could heal and resolve it. I cried when I read *Co-Dependent No More* by Melody Beattie. I thought, *I'm such a mess. How am I going to get out of this?* I felt disheartened, forlorn, and lost.

Up until then, I only identified myself as a Vice President from my corporate days, not as Amanda — a Spiritual Being having a human expe-rience. And, in that outdated identification, I considered myself a failure.

I was taught to be who I was by people who didn't know who they were. They lived by their own 'shoulds,' and sacrificed their needs, desires, and dreams to appease others and pursue what they thought they wanted. There was a right/wrong, good/bad, and successful/failing way of behav-ing. I became that within me and my own life. I had to get clear on who

I was and what I REAL-ly wanted. I had to unearth my dreams that were deeply buried by my 'shoulds.'

Part of that journey was to discover my True purpose, which was to continue to develop and upgrade the System. This would lead to another part of my purpose which is to help steward individuals to connect on a Soul level and to their own Soul's purpose, passion, and plan, so they express through their zone of genius and Diamond brilliance in ways that create joy and prosperity for them. And ideally, they contribute to others and the world by making a difference through what they share.

When the System came to me, I felt totally shut down, lacked clarity, and was uncertain of who I was and what I even wanted. The System helped me connect on all levels within me, and with the Universe.

I began to work with the Connection Diamond Co-Creation Code every day. I was super committed to getting connected. I even built a twelve-foot diameter on the land I lived on with crystals and stones so I could sit within it and meditate. I needed to get connected to myself, my Guides, and the Divine while being grounded on earth.

During my journey, I became more connected to me, the Divine, and with my Soul's Essence, my Guides, and what I am here to do. I came to understand how the System helps you become more aware of your reason for being here, and the gifts you have to offer. It contains the Codes to help create freedom within you and for your life.

I came to believe in the System because it really works!!! What was 'running' me before, no longer does. I healed my co-dependency once and for all, and so much more that was getting in my way of success ... in life, relationships, health and well-being, spirituality, finances, and business. I live life more fully in Love, joy, peace, abundance, and prosperity. All 5th Dimension qualities.

By approaching the System as your friend and collaborator and working with it makes 'light' of any serious issue. You can look at the Codes, color them, decorate with them, meditate and heal with them, and manifest the life you want to live with them.

The System and the Codes are here to serve YOU and co-create with YOU ... your intentions, dreams, and visions so you reach your Highest Order and your Infinite Diamond Potential and brilliance to thrive and prosper in *all* ways and in *all* aspects of your life.

CHAPTER FIVE

The Evolution of The System & The Councils

Over time, The Diamond Co-Creative System® (the System) expanded and evolved just as we do and just as the Divine and the Universe does because all is Infinite. There were nine Universal Diamond Co-Creation Codes which originated in Atlantis that I initially downloaded in 2001 and began to explore to discover how they help us. They showed me different ways of utilizing them for healing, transformation, and manifestation.

The Universal Manifestation Template

One of the main tools that was developed in the beginning was the Universal Manifestation Template (the Template). It's what changed everything for me!

The first time I used the Template it proved its weight in gold. I placed a logo on the Template for a new business I was starting. The business was centered around helping healers, teachers, and spiritual leaders to market and expand their reach. Within six weeks, everything about the business and the opportunities I had fell away. It was clear that this was not a viable business to help others or sustain myself.

And the message I kept getting as I meditated with, or looked at the Template, was … *It's time for you to put yourself out there. You're the healer and teacher to market, not others.* Due to this clarification, my company, Co-Create Your Success, was born and we've been serving others since 2001.

This Template can assist you to create and manifest within any aspect of your life, personally and professionally. It helps you to focus on what you *really* want and quickens your manifestations.

This powerful manifestation tool helps you to:

- Clarify your intentions and tap into your fullest Potential.
- Clear energetic blocks that get in your way and keep you stuck.
- Create awareness of what may or may not be in your Highest Order.
- Align your energetics so you are a vibrational match to your desires.

It assists you in discovering and activating your gifts so you can fulfill your Soul's destiny. It ignites a spark within you to become and express your authentic Self.

The Template helps you save time, money, and energy. I can't tell you how many times it saved me from being distracted by going down a mis-aligned path or choosing something or someone that could have caused me pain, misery, and heartache.

With the System, you can create an abundance of Love, joy, passion, flow, and so much more. It will Energize, Elevate, and Evolve your life, relationships, health and well-being, financial prosperity, and contribution to the world.

We give this away as a gift to help others manifest what they desire and what they came here to experience and do. This gift is an e-Book that includes the Universal Manifestation Template and how to use it so you can Manifest Your ALL! It's our dedication to you and your Soul's journey. Download your gift at: https://link.cocreateyoursuccess.com/eiyabookmyagift.

The Universal 'L'

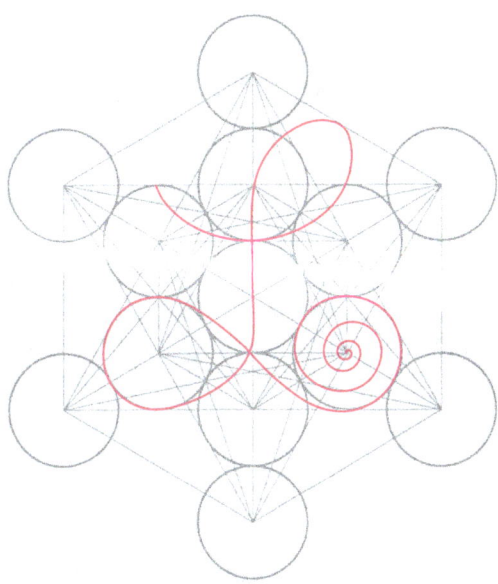

We upgraded the Codes as time went on with the Universal 'L' which is a symbol within many of the Codes. Plus, we added various outer Sacred Geometric designs and a silver, gold, and/or copper metallic bands around the Codes. All of these enhancements upgraded the System into 12th Dimensional energies to help create more Love and unification within each one of us and in the world.

The Universal 'L' can be used as a stand-alone tool to help shift energetics and situations. It is about co-creating with the Universe within the vibrations of Universal Love and Co-Creation to manifest the Highest Order for All. You can utilize it for yourself, or send it to others or out into the world, especially when there are challenges, chaos, natural disasters, discord, or wars. There are also different colors of Universal 'L's that can be used to T.A.M.E. your life … Transform. Align. Manifest. Expand.

The Cosmic Diamond Co-Creation Codes

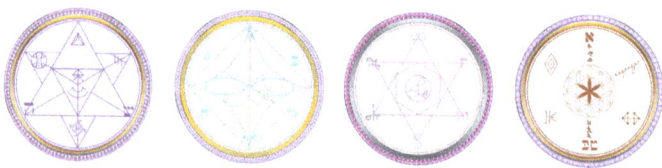

In 2015, four more Codes were channeled in, called the Cosmic Diamond Co-Creation Codes which are infused with new Galactic symbols and energies to assist humanity. A gift from the Universe to us.

This then completed the desire from the System to have thirteen Codes. The number thirteen is an alchemical energy which helps to create a new 5th Dimension foundation and paradigm to operate within. It also assists to create the sacred union of the Divine Feminine and Divine Masculine within and around us … once again to create Oneness and unification of All.

The Cosmic Unification Template

With the addition of the four Cosmic Codes, the Cosmic Unification Template was created. This was a step up for the System to facilitate your ascension process. It assists you to raise your frequencies so you can embody more of your Soul's Essence and energies. Remember, ascension is about 'lightening up' within all your Energy Bodies and in life.

Then COVID hit. As the world came to a screeching halt there was so much fear running rampant. And there was so much unknown as to what we were really dealing with on so many levels: our health, our emotional and mental well-being, our spirituality, our finances, and the pervasive impact COVID was having within our lives.

I began a daily inquiry and asked, "How can I help? How can the System help? What can we do together to heal COVID and what's happening in the world?"

I would walk down to the San Franscico Bay with my dog, Griffin, early in the morning when no one was out. I would sit by the water and be with the Guides and the System. As I consistently did this, new ways of utilizing the System came forward, so it was simpler and easier to use with increased potency and acceleration of our healing, transformation, and evolution.

The Elevation Codes

They first began with downloading the Elevation Codes. The power of the Elevation Codes was beyond what I experienced before. And, of course, there were thirteen Elevation Codes. Each Elevation Code is a combination of two single Diamond Co-Creation Codes.

Each one is used for different purposes, as represented by their names and numerological vibrations, which give you clues as to the one(s) to use. When the single Codes collaborate and co-create together as an Elevation Code, their strength and potency are ten-fold that of a single Code. It is when two or more are gathered in the midst of the Divine, so much more can be created.

When we finally could move about in the summer of 2020, I was guided to go to Mt. Shasta. I was meditating at the same place on the mountain in which I downloaded the Cosmic Codes. As I sat there amid the forest, the Unification Council of 12 presented themselves. This Council began the process of bringing in more teachings and energies about our ascension journey and the unification process that must occur in each one of us if the world is to change and uplevel into a 5th Dimension way of BE-ing and DO-ing.

The Ascension Codes

In the fall, they began to give me the Ascension Codes and again, there were thirteen of them. The Ascension Codes are a combination of four single Diamond Co-Creation Codes from the System connected by a Diamond in the middle, with a circle that links them together. The *Diamond* provides its brilliant High 33rd (Christ-grid Consciousness) frequency, and the *circle* offers Infinite energies, where there is no beginning, nor an end.

Each single Code contributes to the sum of the whole with its function, purpose, and vibrational qualities and becomes exponential in what it creates when combined with other Codes. Thus, by combining four single Codes, it isn't simply 4X the energy; it is actually 44X the power in generating transformation and results.

The Ascension Codes accelerate your transformation, evolution, and ascension into 5th Dimensional vibrations and Higher as you tap into 12th Dimensional Unity consciousness and Oneness. They can help you to attain and sustain your Higher frequencies of Divine Love, joy, passion, flow, and prosperity in all of who you are and do.

As new information continued to come in, I kept asking how else the System could be of service, especially as we came out of the pandemic. There were so many consequences that were affecting us … physically, emotionally, mentally, spiritually, and even financially; many were reevaluating their lives, their relationships, their jobs or their businesses, and what was next for them. Many were impacted by the virus itself if they contracted it and also if someone had chosen to get the vaccine; there were long-term effects created from each scenario.

The Guides had told me there were SOUL-tions with the System, but they had to wait until the time that people were ready to acknowledge what had occurred and wanted assistance. It was in 2022 that two new configurations and techniques were downloaded which utilized the Ascension Codes.

The Transfiguration Ascension Code

The Transfiguration Ascension Code, with its Transformation Protocol, is unique in that it combines six Ascension Codes to provide healing and transformation. The Ascension Codes accelerate your process to heal and realign your cellular structure, Chakras, Energy Bodies, and Energetic Matrix to your original Sacred Geometric Divine blueprint of Love. It assists in reconnecting, or expanding your connection, with the Universal Source energy of Divine Love as part of your evolutionary and ascension process.

The Transfiguration Ascension Code and Protocol can be used for a variety of purposes. If you …

- find yourself needing to boost and balance your Immune System, due to the continuous presence of viruses and other environmental stresses.
- currently have COVID with short-term effects or have been exposed to someone with COVID.
- have had COVID or you may be dealing with how it compromised your health with long COVID.
- have chosen to be vaccinated and your health has been impacted with its short- or long-term side effects.
- have become ill with the flu, a cold, bronchitis, etc.
- have developed a chronic condition.
- have been diagnosed with a disease.
- are in the midst of your ascension process of:
  - raising your frequencies within your Chakras and Energy Bodies.
  - transcending your Physical Body from dense carbon-based ⇢ your Diamond 'Light' Body.
  - shifting your consciousness is from lack/fear-based ⇢ Prosperity/Love/5D ⇢ Oneness and Unity.

And, if you are committed to your ascension process and/or committed to healing and returning to your vibrant health and well-being, then the Transfiguration Ascension Code and Transformation Protocol can assist you.

I used the Transfiguration Ascension Code when I contracted COVID in 2023. Due to my ability to see and feel energy, I could not believe how insidious the virus was in attacking my body, mind, and spirit. It kept trying to disconnect me from the connection I have with the Divine, my

Guides, and my Soul. I found this Code extremely helpful and profound in keeping me connected.

It was a battle of a lifetime but of course Love prevailed and so did my will to deepen and strengthen my connection. It ended up being a part of my own ascension journey.

The Matrix of Oneness

Then came the motherlode, so to speak. The Council combined all thirteen Ascension Codes to create the Matrix of Oneness.

The Matrix of Oneness represents the ability to be in Community ... Common Unity. The values of honor, respect, and absolute Divine Love are the foundation of True community. There is a Love of one another, no matter what (even if you disagree). There is acceptance of diversity, which becomes inclusive. There is harmony, grace, and gratitude that is exuded.

By utilizing the Matrix of Oneness, you can be a steward of uniting humanity through the vibrations of ALL ... Absolute (Abundant) Love & Light. As you heal and transform the past and your old conditioning and programming, you become One with your Soul's Essence and Divine Love. In doing so, you share the vibrations of Oneness and ALL with others and throughout the world.

The Matrix of Oneness is a stand-alone tool, or it can be combined with any other Elevation Code or the Transfiguration Ascension Code. It can be utilized for the healing, transformation, expansion, and evolution of your cellular structure, your Chakras and Energy Bodies, and your consciousness to activate, attract, and hold more Diamond Light and shift you into your Diamond 'Light' Body ... your crystalline Divinity.

The 12th Dimension purpose of the Matrix of Oneness:

- Gives you the ability to bring more Diamond Light within your cellular structure and Physical Body.
- Provides a pathway to unify Love within you so you can uplevel into your Diamond 'Light' Body.
- Assists with the expression of Oneness within yourself, as well as with others.
- Creates unification between the Masculine and the Feminine within and in the world.
- Helps to uplift the egoic mind into the Divine Mind with Soul-aligned energies.
- Generates unification of diversity within inclusivity, thus "All is One."
- Operates from 5th Dimension vibrations and intentions for the Highest Order of All.
- To create the harmony of Oneness and Unity consciousness on earth and within humanity.

Many travel around the world and bury the Matrix of Oneness in the earth as they do ceremony with it to invoke the healing of our planet and Oneness and unification within humankind and the earth. It has been used to correct earth ley lines and to infuse and activate Love, peace, and harmony for the greatest good for All.

At the end of 2022 I was on Mt. Shasta again, another Council presented themselves. This was the Galactic Priestess of Light Council to help us bring in the Divine Feminine aspect of unification. If you were to visualize either of the Councils ... the Unification Council of 12 are tall light beings with a blue hue and the Priestess Council who are also tall have a pink hue to them in which there are twelve of them as well.

The message from the Councils was they wanted now to be known as the Council of ALL bringing the two Councils together. By working with them as one Council, they are bringing in the sacred union of the Divine Masculine and the Divine Feminine, so we all emerge in the Oneness of ourselves as well with others.

Their mission is to impart new teachings through the 5th Dimension Elevation Principles which utilize the Elevation Codes and Protocols. These have been taught through our *Evolve Your ALL 5th Dimension Mentorship* program since the end of 2022. And now you can experience it for yourself in this book.

The 5th Dimension Principles and Elevation Codes from The Diamond Co-Creative System® will help you with the transition from the 3rd to the 4th to the 5th Dimension. They will help you to expand into a Higher consciousness and new way of BE-ing. You can Consciously Choose to operate, create, and live within the vibrations of the 5th Dimension and maintain a life built on these Higher frequency qualities. We invite you to Evolve Into Your ALL ...

As you go through each of the 5th Dimension Elevation Principles with their Codes and Protocols, there are also Universal Laws we share to help you implement the Principles. Universal Laws are not manmade; they are spiritual principles guided by the Divine and they are Universal regardless of what others think. For example, you cannot argue with the Law of Gravity. It is because it is.

The Universal Laws will help you better understand the 5th Dimension Elevation Principle and support the why you want to incorporate and embody the Principle within any aspect of your life. We also share crystals or gemstones that will enhance your experience with each of the Principles. And the Council of ALL impart their wisdom with a message to help guide you with the integration of each Principle into your life.

CHAPTER SIX

The Elevation Codes & Their Protocols

FREEDOM

Expression

Power

An Elevation Code is a combination of two Diamond Co-Creation Codes from The Diamond Co-Creative System®. Each Elevation Code is ten-fold the potency of a single Code, which increases its effectiveness and power to assist with the healing and transformation process, as well as your creation and manifestation of possibilities to elevate into your MORE and evolve into your ALL ... Absolute (Abundant) Light and Love.

Elevation Protocols have been designed to make it easier and simpler to utilize the Elevation Codes of The Diamond Co-Creative System®. The name of the Protocol gives you the intention of what each Protocol can provide you, or your client. It reveals what its purpose is and how it can help you.

So, what is a Protocol? Think of it as a medical treatment plan but in this case, it is an energetic meta (spiritual)-physical treatment plan. Medically, you receive a Protocol to use when you have a physical ailment or condition to help you heal and to achieve optimal health. Well, with the Elevation Code Protocols, they address not only what's going on physically but also what type of results in your life that you're unhappy with, by confronting the emotional, mental, and spiritual aspects of an issue, concern, or intention as well.

An Elevation Code Protocol helps to discover what may be energetically blocking you or what may be energetically incongruent and out of alignment, so you may resolve and complete old energetic patterns, conditioning, and programming. As you do so, you can create a new energetic alignment and algorithm to then manifest a new outcome.

The Elevation Codes along with the Protocols help you to align with your original Sacred Geometry of Divine Love and the Infinite, so you can thrive and prosper in this lifetime. Because the System is based on Sacred Geometry, it makes it easier for you to realign with your original Divine blueprint of Love and embody more of your Soul's Essence.

You can simply activate the Elevation Code or the Protocol with what you have identified as your intention and desire to transform, co-create, and manifest. It will do its magic as you focus upon your intention. With its Divine-cell Consciousness, it knows what you Truly want and need (even if you don't know).

The Elevation Code Protocol is a two-part process. The *CCC ... Clear, Cleanse, and Calibrate* portion of the Protocol helps to release dense lower vibration, stuck, or blocked energies within your Chakras and Energy Bodies. As you invoke the Elevation Code(s), imagine them being placed within your Chakras and Energy Bodies that require attention. As you activate the Codes to clear and transmute old energies that no longer serve or work for you, they will *spin counterclockwise* to assist you.

When you are complete with the release and clearing process, the Elevation Codes will come to a still point. You may sense, see, imagine, or feel when they do, which is the indication to move into the second part of the process.

Whenever you release energy, you *always* want to replace, repattern, and recalibrate your energy with Higher frequencies (Love and 5th Dimension or Higher vibrations), your Highest Order, and your Infinite

Diamond Potential. You also want to invoke the vibrations or state of BE-ing that is opposite of what you released, i.e., from sadness to joy, from fear to Love, from unworthiness to worthiness, from scarcity to abundance, from lack to prosperity, and so on. Do not leave a void after your release.

You can fill the void with new energies by activating the Elevation Codes within the *EEE ... Energize, Elevate, and Evolve* portion of your healing session or meditation. The Codes may be a combination of some of the same and also different Codes, or even an entirely different Code or set of Codes; follow your intuition and Divine's guidance, or use the Protocols we provide in each of the 5th Dimension chapters which makes it easier for you.

Envision the Elevation Codes being placed within *all* of your Chakras and Energy Bodies. The Codes will *spin clockwise* to repattern and recalibrate your Chakras and Energy Bodies, bringing them back into current time and upleveling them into the Higher frequencies that the Codes hold. This helps to align your energies to what (and whom) is in your Highest Order and the abilities to fulfill your Infinite Diamond Potential.

Plus, when you release the dense energies, you have created space for your Soul's Essence to flow back into the crevasses of your energy fields. This assists you to embody more of your Soul's energies so it can radiate throughout you and express through you.

You can always activate and *EEE* the Elevation Codes anytime throughout the day to assist you. This may be done to boost, reinforce, or realign your energies. Be sure when you activate them, do so with intention.

CCC and EEE Suggested Verbiage:

CCC: (Name of Elevation Codes) Activate, Activate, Activate, Clear, Cleanse, and Calibrate, Calibrate, Calibrate, 44 Times Divine Source Speed at the 44th Power to Purify, Purify, Purify, my Chakras (or a specific Chakra) and Energy Bodies (or a specific Energy Body), so they can (state your intention) within the 5th Dimension or beyond and to my Highest Order and Infinite Diamond Potential.

Violet Flame ... Transmute, Transmute, Transmute, 33 Times Divine Source Speed at the 33rd Power.

EEE: (Name of Elevation Codes) Energize, Energize, Energize, Elevate, Elevate, Elevate, and Evolve, Evolve, Evolve 44 Times Divine Source Speed at the 44th Power, and saturate every cell of my Being, my Chakras, and my Energy Bodies with (your intention) within all aspects of my life and in the 5th Dimension or beyond, and for my Highest Order and fulfillment of my Infinite Diamond Potential.

You may be guided to use different words … trust yourself and what you receive as guidance from your Soul and/or the Divine. As you use the Codes and Protocols more, you will gain more confidence in how to utilize the Codes and Protocols. You can't do it wrong, and you will not harm yourself, or another person, by not saying it perfectly. Remember, it is the purity of your intention and Love that the Elevation Codes and System respond to and assist you and another in the Highest Order.

Elevation Code Protocol Steps:

Step 1. You always begin with the Infinite Divine Breath to ground and center yourself, and to become connected with yourself, Divine Source, and the Infinite Possibilities of the Universe. See Chapter Seven for information and instructions.

Call in Divine Source, your Guides, Angels, and any other Divine Being to assist you. Archangel Michael, St. Germaine, Lord Melchizedek, Metatron, and the Divine beings who overlight The Diamond Co-Creative System®, and the Council of ALL will join you as well due to you utilizing the System in your process.

Archangel Michael assists with past lives and cord-cutting, and Metatron will help to remove old energetic grids, chips, or cords as he works alongside Michael. It is also the Sacred Geometry of Metatron's Cube on which the System is built. Lord Melchizedek is a great spiritual Master of alchemy and Sacred Geometry and is said to sit at the right hand of the Divine to impart Divine Guidance and create unification through the weave and patterns of Love and Light. St. Germaine brings you the Violet Flame which transmutes negative and low frequency energies and repatterns the energy back to Love and other Higher frequencies.

Step 2. After you are grounded, centered, and connected, you will move into your metaphysical chamber which helps you to feel safe and relaxed; the chamber is in a Higher Dimension and accessed through the golden door within your heart. As you imagine or see the golden door, open it up, and step through it onto a lighted pathway that leads you to your metaphysical chamber. You may even have an Angel or Guide greet you and take you to your chamber.

This chamber is all about you so it will be what you want; it is a sacred space reflecting your beauty and brilliance. Some see it as a brightly lit vast space, a place, a garden, a field, the woods, a beach. Whatever it is, it is perfect for you.

Your Guides and the Divine Beings that you invoked will join you there and invite you to sit or lay down within this space; it could be to sit in a chair designed just for you or to lay upon a beautiful rose quartz or crystal table. Or if in nature, there may be a bench or blanket surrounded by flowers and fairies. Let your vision or imagination guide you. The Guides will then encircle you and hold the energy for your transformation.

State your intentions and bring forth what you feel needs to be healed and transformed. As you do so, what you consciously know to be True will come forth, and what is at a cellular level and in the subconscious will also arise. You may or may not be aware of what is locked in your subconscious but with your intention to heal and transform, it will be revealed and addressed.

Step 3. Begin with the *CCC … Clear, Cleanse, and Calibrate* portion of the Protocol. You will invoke the Elevations Codes to assist your Chakras and Energy Bodies; these may be specific ones that you have identified that need assistance, or all of them. When you do so, envision, see, sense, or feel them as holograms being placed where necessary and even around you. Everyone is different in how they experience this; there is no right or wrong way. And the Codes will go wherever they are needed so you don't need to know how or what they are doing or to control the process.

The Elevation Codes that are named will *spin counterclockwise* first to help with the release and clearing of energies that no longer serve you within your Chakras and Energy Bodies. They will also layer upon one another as they collectively work together to assist you. You can also utilize the Violet Flame to help transmute and purify energies, so they can realign to the vibration to Divine Love.

When the *CCC* process is finished, you may see, sense, feel, or imagine the Elevation Codes come to still point which is a signal that the *CCC* is complete. The Codes will do this on their own, because of their Divine-cell Consciousness … they know what you need and want. Again, you don't have to control the process; ask your egoic mind to let go, allow, and *trust* the process. Understand, you can do no harm to yourself or another with the Codes as they are protected and will not allow any negative use or harm to come to you.

Step 4. Once the *CCC* is complete, you will begin to upgrade, realign, and recalibrate the energies within your Chakras and Energy Bodies with the *EEE … Energize, Elevate, and Evolve* portion of the Protocol. When you activate the Elevation Codes this time, they will *spin clockwise* to align and shift the vibrational frequencies of your Chakras and Energy Bodies to Love and upgraded 5th Dimension vibrations or beyond. The Codes will calibrate and align your Chakras and Energy Bodies to present time, and to your Highest Order and Infinite Diamond Potential.

During the *EEE*, allow yourself to receive and embody more of your Soul's Essence. Invite your Soul to fill and energize each of your Chakras and Energy Bodies. Many times, it looks like a beautiful golden white light clockwise spiral coming down your Chakra ladder, filling each Chakra then expanding out into your Energy Bodies and into your energetic matrix. Again, this can only occur because you have cleared the dense energies that no longer serve you; you've created energetic space for your Soul's energies to fill.

Step 5. When you feel complete, give gratitude to yourself, to Divine Source and your Spirit Guides, and to anyone that was part of your healing and transformation. You may want to anchor in the feeling of what you experienced, or anchor in the new sensations and vibrations of what the Protocol helped you access; you can do so by placing your hands on your heart or somewhere on your body. Remember what it feels like and take an imprint of it in your mind, heart, and body.

Then slowly come back into the space you are in and gently open your eyes. Take an Epsom salt bath within 24 hours to help with your assimilation and integration process. You typically will notice within 72 hours or sooner a shift; it may be subtle, or it may seem very profound. The more you do a Protocol, the more you evolve, then it may seem like a big leap in consciousness and in creating new results.

Keep repeating a Protocol until you are in the state of BE-ing and DO-ing that you desire or have manifested the outcomes you want. Each time you use the Protocol, it will yield different experiences, insights, and results.

Continue to utilize a Protocol as often as you are guided. And at times, you may put one aside then come back to it later when you are prompted by your guidance to do so. You may also be guided to combine one or more Protocols depending on what you are working on and want to attain within yourself and in different aspects of your life.

Download a full-size color set of the Elevation Codes at: https://link.cocreateyoursuccess.com/eiyabookresourcehub

CHAPTER SEVEN

Grounding & Centering With the Infinite Divine Breath

The Infinite Divine Breath (or sometimes called the Infinity Breath) is the link in connecting your Body (Heart), Mind, and Soul (Spirit). The Infinite Divine Breath allows them to open to one another and connect with each other and with the Universe. It also creates an etheric bridge between the Physical Body and its other Energy Bodies.

The Infinity Breath connects the etheric/electro-magnetic with the physical/magnetic and lets these energies travel and communicate back and forth. It is the energy interconnection between the spiritual and the physical. It is a process of energy-matter-light integration.

It provides a multi-access opening to multidimensional energies and to the Universal grid network that generates a color-sound resonance to equalize polarities. It gives you access to the doorway of Universal channels and to the Infinite quantum field of the Universe.

The Infinity Breath can be utilized any time: as you go throughout the day, in a meditation, to begin a healing process, or as you start a call or meeting which helps you and others to get grounded, centered, and connected. You can do it standing, sitting, or lying down. The suggestion is to call in Divine Source (or your terminology) and your etheric team of Spirit Guides, Angels, Teachers, Ascended Masters, or whoever they are for you to be there with you.

We encourage you to concentrate on breathing in and out of your mouth with an open relaxed jaw. This assists the Throat — 5th Chakra to be activated and connected with the lower energy systems allowing for emotion ... *energy in motion* to flow. A rhythmic cycle of motion occurs between your Physical Body, your Soul's Essence, and the energy of the Universal Source quantum field of the Infinite.

As you do so, close your eyes (unless you're driving, or need to keep them open) and visualize, imagine, feel, or sense a figure 8, an upright Infinity Sign. The top of the Infinity Sign connects at the top of your head (at the Crown — 7th Chakra), the center point passes through your Heart — 4th Chakra, and the bottom of it connects to the base of your spine (at the Root — 1st Chakra). As you inhale, imagine or see yourself tracing the figure 8 from the bottom up to its top to your Crown, then exhale at the top and trace the breath on the opposite side dropping down to the bottom to your Root. This completes the breath cycle of tracing the entire figure 8.

Repeat this motion of tracing the 8 as you inhale and exhale. It doesn't matter which side it goes up — right or left; allow it to drop down on the opposite side so you trace the entire figure 8 with your breath on the inhale and exhale.

This gives your egoic mind a new job to trace the Infinity Sign with the breath instead of trying to figure out what's going on and getting in your way.

Let your breath fall into a natural rhythm, don't push or pull the breath, let it flow naturally. As you go along, the Infinity Sign may shift position, or even multiply; whatever happens, it is in Divine Order.

Now you can ground, center, and further connect by sending a beam of light from your Heart down the Chakra ladder to the base of your spine at the Root Chakra, then see it dividing into three beams of light with one going down through the perineum and the other two down your legs traveling to the center of Mother Earth — Gaia to connect with her and the crystalline grid. Gaia's crystalline grid is already in the 7th Dimension which is Creator energy and helps you claim that within you.

As the beams of light connect to the crystalline grid, the two beams of light that came down your legs will bounce back up bringing the beautiful nurturing and grounding energies of Gaia, and the crystalline energies of the grid back up through the soles of your feet, up your legs, and up into your Chakra ladder filling each of your lower Chakras — 1st through the 7th. The center light beam through your perineum is your grounding cord and will not bring up energy.

Then send a beam of light from your heart up your Chakra ladder to the 12th Chakra 300 feet above your head and beyond to connect with the Heavens. As you send a beam of light up into the Heavens to the great Central Sun–Divine Source, you will connect with Divine Love and Diamond Light as well as your Divine birthrights of compassion, grace, wisdom, power, peace, abundance, prosperity, and gratitude.

Allow yourself to receive these energies as they flow down the Chakra ladder to fill each of your Chakars — 12th down through your 1st and to the 10th Chakra below your feet. Allow for the energies of Heaven and earth to pass back and forth, lighting up your Chakra Ladder, creating a connection between Universal Source energy and Mother Earth within you, through you, and around you so you are grounded and centered within these High frequency energies.

Then ask for these energies to flow out from your Heart Chakra and expand into your Physical Body to infuse more Divine Love, Diamond Light, and crystalline grid energy into your organs, muscles, tissues, glands, bones, and systems. Next, expand this energy into your Auric field (the golden egg shape around you) to raise your frequencies and seal it with a golden white light as well add a layer of the Violet Flame from St. Germaine to protect and strengthen your field.

Bring into your Third Eye — 6th Chakra a vision or connect within your Heart — 4th Chakra to call forth your intention for the day, for what activity you are doing, or for what you would like to manifest ... ask your Guides and the Universe to assist you throughout the day.

Remember, you don't have to live life or manifest what you want alone. You always have an etheric Divine team (the Divine, your Spirit Guides, Angels, Ascended Masters, etc.) who assist you, but you must ask for their help!

Focus on your desire and feel into it, even if it you can't see *how* it will be physically manifested, or upset or disappointed with what's not yet manifested. Let go of focusing on what's not and replace it with the vibrations of appreciation and gratitude. Let go of you trying to make it happen and let the Universe support and help you. Thank the Universe for fulfilling your request and see it as being done so … this or something even MORE or better!

The 5th Dimension and Infinite Possibilities vibrations that the Universe offers are always the pathways to co-creating and evolving into your ALL … Abundant (Absolute) Light & Love!

CHAPTER EIGHT

The 5th Dimension Elevation Principle & Codes of Forgiveness & Peace

The Elevation Principle

Your peace within is created through your Conscious Choice of claiming yourself as a Creator and Co-Creator who desires peace, regardless of what has occurred.

You co-create *everything* and *everyone* in your life; there is always a purpose and gift in each creation. This includes any situation and person who becomes incongruent with who you are as a radiant BE-ing of Light and Love, and with what you Truly desire to create, express, and manifest.

The feelings, thoughts, words, and acts of forgiveness open the doorway to True peace within and frees you to move about your life in the flow of LOVE ... Living Only (One) Vibrant Energy and JOY ... Journey Onward Yielding.

As you let go and yield into your ALL ... Absolute (Abundant) Light and Love, you have more and more opportunities to play, operate, and create in the 5th Dimension of FLOW ... Freely Living (within your) Own Wisdom.

As you accept that you are a Creator and Co-Creator, you can now 'own' the wisdom that you hold. It is the knowledge you've gained through all your experiences that then becomes wisdom.

As you've learned, grown, healed, transformed, and continue to evolve through your experiences, all becomes Wisdom. You hold that innate Wisdom at a Soul level as well as within your Physical Body.

A Message from the Council of ALL

Greetings Dear Ones,

We ask that you Love, honor, and respect who you are and all that you've experienced. We do so for you, and so shall you, in order to expand into and stabilize in the 5th Dimension. Peace is a vibration in which it opens doorways for you to experience more Love and Light.

You cannot hold the elements of discord and lack of forgiveness and expect to radiate Light and Love. We beseech you to find forgiveness within first, then you can do so with others.

In this, you will discover and embody the peace you seek. We hold that you become peace.

We love you so. Blessed Be.

Gem/Crystal for the Principle: Amethyst

Amethyst is a stone of spirituality and contentment which transmutes lower energies into Higher frequencies. It helps to facilitate healing and transformation. It assists to balance the Emotional, Mental, and Physical Bodies. Amethyst provides stability, strength, invigoration, and peace.

It also assists in the gathering and assimilation of new ideas. It is a crystal of abundance and prosperity!

It vibrates to the #3: joy, fun, creativity, and the trinity.

The Universal Law of Forgiveness

Imagine waking up from a nap or coming out of meditation and there's a glow about you, brought about by lifting the burdens of the past and the heaviness in your heart. You are no longer weighed down with pain, grief, anger, or resentment, and your spirit feels free to live once again. You feel an energy which allows you the freedom to Love and co-create from your brilliant Soul's Essence! You may ask, "how can this be, and how can I continue to create this for myself in my life?"

It is through the Law of Forgiveness that the gates open to the Kingdom of Heaven. It's not the Heaven above, but rather it's the "Heaven on Earth," that you can create within you by fully embracing the vibration of Love … Living Only (One) Vibrant Energy. If you lived in a world in which only Love and acceptance existed, would you need the Law of Forgiveness? Of course, you would not.

Since you're not in the constant and consistent state of Love, forgiveness is usually required at some point in your life because of the upset, anger, disappointment, judgment, or blame of yourself, others, or a situation. When upset, anger, or disappointment is held, and regurgitated repeatedly, then Love, compassion, and acceptance cannot exist. When judgment and blame occur, separation is created, and Love is no longer present.

When understanding, acceptance, and Love is present, there is no longer the vibration or feeling of separation, or even the need for forgiveness. Forgiveness is not about condoning what occurred, but rather accepting "what is, is." Not forgiving yourself, or another, will continue to only hurt you, not the other.

Forgiveness is the gift and the Highest form of Love that you can give to yourself and others. It is the allowance for yourself to learn, heal, grow, and move on from the experience. Forgiveness provides a pathway of understanding and honoring of 'why' the experience occurred and the ability to let it go.

It's not about forgetting what happened but about accepting what was and what will no longer be. Have you heard, "I forgive you, but I'll never forget what you've done," but it's said with such anger, resentment, malice, and vengeance? This is not True forgiveness.

Forgiveness cannot be only a mental process through rationalization, thoughts, and words. Empty words or gestures will not bring you peace. Forgiveness is a tool to let go of the past, but for it to work, it must be *held and felt* within your heart and *given* from your heart. Forgiveness allows you to access the vibrations, feelings, and knowingness of Love, compassion, and acceptance within all parts of your BE-ing.

You may want to hold onto your hurt, anger, the need to be right, or justification about how wrong you or they were, but it will not provide you with the freedom to create something new, or to create peace within.

The lack of forgiveness creates grief, despair, resentment, regret, and anger within your heart and mind. It drains your energy and takes away your life force. It skews your perception of what's really True, which leads you to make assumptions and decisions based on falsehoods. This generates unhappiness, frustration, and lack of fulfillment within your own life, not theirs. It does not affect them, it affects you.

The wound, or pain, from the past is an *incomplete energetic cycle.* If it is left unresolved and not completed, it is perpetuated in other relationships and situations. It can eventually manifest as physical illness and dis-ease within any one your Energy Bodies ... Physical, Emotional, Mental, or Spiritual. It keeps you stuck in the past with an inability to move forward.

Remember, you co-create *everything* and *everyone* in your life, whether you want to acknowledge this or not. And, whether you are willing to take responsibility for what is occurring or not. It is the Universal Law of Cause and Effect that requires you to be accountable and responsible for what you create.

Many times, you invite (consciously and subconsciously) people and situations into your life, so you may co-create, experience, learn, heal, grow, or fulfill a karmic debt and complete the karma. The people that arrive in your life or the situations that occur could be due to one, or all, of these reasons.

If so, you are playing out karmic relationships, or Soul agreements. Karmic relationships are based on balancing a deficit, while a Soul agreement is created to fulfill a common purpose.

Karma is a cycle in which two Souls need to complete an energetic exchange or specific lesson from the past; in many cases one owes the other and there is a payback needed to complete the karma. If the person who owes does not fulfill their part of the karma, you can still choose to let it go, move on, and complete the energetic cycle yourself.

A Soul agreement is agreed to by both parties to assist what one, or both, want to co-create and experience. It could be beneficial to one or both parties.

Both karma or Soul agreements can be extremely gratifying, productive, and rewarding, or they can be quite challenging. It depends on the nature of either, and the maturity and perspective of the individuals involved. If either is about healing, or completing the past for a particular person, there is usually some sort of upset or judgment with yourself or one another, thus forgiveness is a necessary part of the process.

Within this type of experience, typically one is deemed right or wrong, good or bad, rather than the acceptance of just what is, is. There is a comparison that one truth is better than or less than, one is more valued while the other is undervalued. Understanding the True sense of Nature, all truths are actually the sum of the whole ... there is the Divine Truth at the core of any experience.

It's important that both of whom are involved 'own' what is going on for them and do their part. However, one person may not do so and will not do their work. If this is the case, focus on you and do your own personal work so you can fulfill your part of the Soul agreement or karmic debt, or complete the karmic cycle, and then move on.

Forgiveness of another (or yourself) restores the Truth of one's own being.
It brings freedom, transparency, and the restoration of life.
When your life is transparent, you are free, wise, and of service to all.
Glenda Green — *The Keys of Jeshua*

Forgiveness is about moving away from the dead, unproductive, or draining energy of discord or past pain, to the present of where you and the other are today. Did you learn, heal, and grow from your experience?

The past is a record that can be utilized for discernment, but it's not to keep yourself or another in a 'box' which is no longer True or relevant and no longer serves either of you. Are you looking at the gifts that it brings you?

Honoring and accepting the unique truth of both, you create a bridge for each to freely co-create and live your own Soul's purpose and path. As each person is unique, so is one's path and journey … my path and journey are not yours, and yours are not mine. It is honoring the path and journey of each from which freedom is created and expressed and peace within is felt.

Let's break down the word Forgiveness:

For: the purpose of; by reason of; in honor of

Give: to present voluntarily without expecting a return; to apply fully or freely, to pledge, to make a gift, or to contribute

My Forgiveness Exploration

◊   What is my definition of Forgiveness?

◊   How do I give and receive Forgiveness?

◊   What's the difference in completing Forgiveness with feeling versus just thinking or saying it?

◊   Identify the wounds and pain of the past which create the same types of situations and people in your life.

◊   List who and what that you're not able or are willing to let go of. Examples: your past mistakes, failures, or judgments and upsets about who you are, your body, your health, your money, types of relationships you choose or are in, your work, etc. and the different situations or stories you have with other people. Let's explore …

    With My Self and well-being (your acceptance, Love, honor, respect, and care of yourself):

    With my health and body:

    With others:

    With a significant other:

    With my family or a family member:

    With my friend(s):

    With my co-workers or business partners:

    With the Universe:

    With my money and finances:

    With my mistakes or failures:

    Within a situation …

        At home:

        At work or within my business:

◊   What are the vibrations of Forgiveness versus hanging onto the past?

◊   What does it feel like when you do let go and Forgive? When you don't?

    Lack of Forgiveness feels like …

    Forgiveness feels like …

◊   It's important to know you don't continue to do the same thing, create the same situations or people in your life, without having a payoff (getting something out of it even if it's not what you want, or is perceived seemingly as a negative result). This can give you the "why" you won't let go and Forgive. So, what are my payoffs to keep holding on to the anger, upset, resentment, resignation, etc. I am feeling _____? Break it down by person and/or situation.

My Peace Exploration

◊   How do I define Peace?

◊   How committed am I to have Peace within me and within my life?

◊   How does Peace show up in my life and how does it not?

◊   What or whom do I allow to take me out of my Peace?

◊   How often am I in Peace and how often am I not?

◊   Where does my lack of forgiveness take me out of my sense of Peace?

The Universal Law of Divine Union

Have you ever wondered why your life is out of balance? Why are tasks and projects a struggle, or never seem to be completed? Why don't your relationships really work for you? Why are you unhappy and unfulfilled in your life and/or career? Have you felt like something seems off, not operating in sync, and not connected?

If any of these questions apply to you, then we invite you to consider the dynamics of your energy within, and the possibility to create balance and peace within. The Universal Law of Divine Union can answer so many of these questions and provide you with SOUL-utions as well. Remember, everything is energy, and you in turn are a combination of energetic dynamics and patterns.

The Divine Union is two-fold. The first is the union is between you and your I AM Presence — your Divine-cell consciousness of Love. And the second is the Sacred Divine Union of Masculine and Feminine energetics within you.

There is actually no separation between you and Divine Source, spirit and matter, and Father Sky and Mother Earth. However, due to past pain and conditioning, most people believe in or feel separation rather than a sense of Oneness.

Divine Union requires this connection to Oneness and a state of honoring yourself, and whomever or whatever enters your life. With this honoring, magic occurs that allows you to feel the Divine Source connection within and its Divine Love. With honor, there is acceptance, in which you are free of conditions and attachments to your expectations. Divine Union occurs and pours within your energy fields and into your Bodies of Consciousness (Energy Bodies) ... Physical, Emotional, Mental, and Spiritual.

As you release and heal your fears, traumas, wounds, and pain, you transcend separation and begin to truly become the Divine Union within. You create a union between your heart (Feminine) and mind (Masculine).

You manage the egoic mind and uplift it into the Divine Mind, rather than the ego trying to control you so you feel safe, secure, and protected.

You begin to trust the connection and synchronicities of the Universe within your life. Your patterns of fear become something of the past and Sacred Divine Union takes its place. Thus, this develops into a sustainable way of BE-ing and DO-ing.

The second part of Divine Union is the understanding of your Masculine, Feminine, and Inner Child energetics. Just as we see in Nature the genders of male and female, so do the energetics of the male and female exist within you and within every creation. Your Inner Child energy is sourced from you as you grew up and what he or she holds as his/her experiences.

We each hold Masculine, Feminine, and Inner Child energetics that result in the qualities and vibrations of who we are. Within the Divine Union, they discover one another and learn how to co-create and work together, rather than feel separated and alone. They learn to how to Love, honor, and respect one another.

If any aspect of you is fearful of the other, in competition, not trusting itself or another, not connected to or communicating with each other, or not working and co-creating together, then you become out of balance. For balance to occur, the Divine Union is necessary.

Notice the qualities of your relationships around you whether it is with a Beloved, friends, co-workers, or merely someone walking down the street. It doesn't matter if the relationship is female to female, female to male, male to male, or male to female, both aspects of the Masculine and Feminine are present.

Observe and watch the dynamics of your relationships. Is there conflict, fear, or just plain unhappiness with others? Are your relationships flowing, smooth, loving, joyous, prosperous, and free of pain, or is there the need for power, control, and/or protection?

Your relationship will always reflect to you what is *really* going on within you. These reflections are your clues and the indications of what is out of balance if you are *reactive*. They show you the energetics that need to be addressed and the desire of what wants to be healed within your Bodies of Consciousness.

This is especially true if you are in a Beloved, or some sort of close intimate relationship, since we all tend to attract a person who will help us to correct the imbalances of the Masculine, Feminine, and Inner Child within. This also applies to all relationships whether you are straight or gay. If you're not in a Beloved relationship, then observe your other significant relationship(s) including friends, or those within your family, workplace, or business.

If you are *neutral* and don't feel any trigger or attachment to certain outcomes, even if a relationship isn't working for you or there's a conflict, you will feel peace within. You will know your next steps and come from a 5th Dimensional way of BE-ing and take Soul-aligned actions.

The Universal Law of Polarities

The Universal Law of Polarities show us that everything is dual and has poles. All are its pairs of opposite and the opposites are identical in nature, but different in degree. For example, the energy of Love is really the same energy of fear, but quite different in the degree in which it is perceived and felt. One can be hysterically crying, and in the next moment be hysterically laughing. Same energy, different polarity and different frequency.

It's only the experience of the degree of the vibration (or you could say the degree of separation) that differentiates the perception and label. We can Consciously Choose how we perceive the experience of the energy while other times we may have a subconscious reaction.

Everything has polarity and without the Law of Polarities, light, dark, or electric, magnetic, or expansion, denseness could not exist. Each energy has its polar opposite effects. The Law of Cause and Effect is closely connected to this Law. The cause creates the effect.

The fundamental patterns of nature exist in balance, and it will continue to adjust to create the balance within itself. For example, the swinging of the pendulum is representative of this balance. It will always return to where it began — in the middle. The balance is created by swinging to the right, then to the left, and eventually comes to rest at center point, the balance point. Reach this balance and you will be at peace.

Now, what does that have to do with our lives and creations, and how does it affect them? It has everything to do with it!

Let's begin to understand it through the co-creative process of the Masculine and Feminine energies. They are polar opposites of each other, yet you cannot create one without the other. You may be out of balance within each of the energies on some level, but both aspects of the polarities are required to manifest, i.e., thought + feelings = physical form.

As within the Law of Polarities, neither Masculine nor Feminine energies are more or less important, both must be present. Again, one could show up more prevalent than the other due to the past and conditioning, programming, or patterns. Many were taught to lead with the Masculine energy even if you're a woman; it was the way to get ahead and to be successful in society's way of thinking and doing.

But each aspect has its own power and strength that contributes to your life and manifestations. To maximize the potential of your creations, a blending of both as well as an honoring, acceptance, and respect of what each 'brings to the table' is important.

In the True balance of nature, it is not a paradigm in which the Masculine is more powerful or important, or the Feminine energy is less than or weaker than the Masculine. The qualities and aspects they both contribute to and the level at which they are at is the key to your success.

It's not that we are just male or female in a physical human being body; we have both energetics that live within us. You could say that you have your own male/female dynamic that is occurring within you. Ideally you want to create a Sacred marriage ... a Divine Union between these aspects of yourself so you feel Love, strong, and powerful within.

When you have a Loving, compassionate, and supportive relationship within yourself, it reflected by the beautiful dance of your Masculine and Feminine within weaving their energies together as they embrace the mastery of one another. It is the mergence and emergence of the Divine Union which creates flow and balance.

When your Masculine and Feminine are out of balance, it can cause a great deal of stress, worry, and anxiety affecting your peace of mind and well-being. It can create incongruencies and out of alignments with what you really want in your life, relationships, and even in your career or business.

When you're not embracing, Loving, honoring, accepting, and respecting what each aspect offers, then an out of balance occurs and the outcomes are less than ideal. You cannot reach your ultimate Diamond

Potential if you don't acknowledge the contribution each aspect provides within the co-creative process of your life and creations. In other words, you will not enjoy the ride.

We have seen this show up time and again when someone is only allowing the Masculine to dictate their lives. They have difficulty with emotion, they don't follow their intuition, and they're always on the go. They must be doing something and be productive all the time to feel good about themselves, yet they don't necessarily achieve their goals and continue to chase after what they think they need and want. They may be close-minded, rigid, and structured. And, they definitely are not having fun!

Most likely their relationships are not working on some level and are dysfunctional with power and control issues at the forefront. There is neediness and co-dependency looking for Love and acceptance (in all the wrong places) as well as on a 'hunt' to create safety and security at all costs, including sacrifice of Self and others.

The opposite effect can also occur if the Feminine is in control. She could be in the midst of gathering lots of information, very emotional, and so expansive that she's not grounded. Since she is not the aspect that creates structure and form, more and more confusion and chaos ensue leading to a lack of manifestation and results. The Masculine gets frustrated because he cannot 'do,' provide, or protect, which are his functions.

Trust is essential to build between both. As the Feminine gathers information and receives inspiration and ideas from within, from your Soul, and the Divine, she intuitively guides the Masculine to organize and shape the energy into structure and form. This Divine Union dance is a 5th Dimensional way of BE-ing and DO-ing which creates a beautiful and powerful flow of resonance, synchronicity, and unification.

The ultimate is when the Masculine and Feminine are in a place of cooperation, collaboration, and co-creation (5th Dimensional qualities), then magic and miracles occur in each moment and each day. Both the Masculine and Feminine are inspired, motivated, and energized as well as they love, admire, and adore the mastery of each other with the unique talents, abilities, and attributes they offer.

Now, let's add in the Inner Child. When your Inner Child heals the wounds from the past or from your family as you grew up, she/he comes back into alignment with the True nature of yourself … Love. They now carry their original Divine innocence, the curiosity, the imagination, the adventurer, and the discoverer that is innate in Child energy.

The Child brings in the fun and play; you can ask them to join you in your relationships and even when you're working or creating something new which brings in the joy of what you're doing. It's important to notice if your wounded Child is trying to 'run' the show or if your healthy Child is contributing.

How do you do this? Just as in your relationships outside of yourself, you must be open to having honest and authentic communication within yourself and with your aspects. Each aspect needs to take ownership of where they are individually, as well as collectively with each other. They must claim their responsibility for what is created and hold themselves accountable for the manifestations that occur.

When each aspect calls itself out on what is True for them and 'owns' it, they claim back their power because they now know they can change what doesn't work and can do something about it. In that, they can release upset, blame, shame, guilt, victimhood, martyrdom, and judgment about themselves and the other aspects. If each aspect of yourself is not honest with itself, then it cannot be that with the other, which you will also notice to be true in all your relationships to some degree or another.

There is a weave that can occur as Divine co-creations prevail with ease, grace, synchronicity, and flow. It is Truly coming from your inner sense of empowerment when you discern what is working and what is not, not only within the Masculine, Feminine, and Inner Child, but also as a collective. When you do so, a balance of the polarities can be achieved, and the pendulum can come back to a place of peace, serenity, fulfillment, and contentment.

It's your choice to Consciously Choose to create the magical emergence of the Polarities within a powerful, masterful weave and dance of co-creation. And, in that you discover and feel the peace and power within!

Exploration to Create Sacred Divine Union Within

Next Step. Create peace within by allowing your inner aspects to heal, grow, forgive, and express who they Truly are. What can each aspect contribute from the strength and power of their innate qualities and purpose? In the 5th Dimension, what are the ways they can shine and help you stabilize in the Higher frequencies?

Aspects & Qualities of Your Inner Family		
Masculine Energies	**Feminine Energies**	**Child Energies**
God/Male	Goddess/Female	Childlike
Light/Bright	Dark/Void	Fun/Joy/Play
Day/Sun/Summer/Hot	Night/Moon/Winter/Cold	Divine Innocence
Mind/Mental/Thoughts	Heart/Emotional/Feelings	Imaginative
Provider/Protector/Assertive/Action	Receptive/Gatherer/Inward/Quiet	Present Moment
Projector/Outward/Social	Nurturer/Gentle/Introverted	Adventurer/Discovery
Electrical/Sky/Spiritual	Magnetic/Earth/Physical	Exporer/Seeker
Dense/Contractive/Specific/Linear/Hard	Fluid/Expansive/Universal/Circular/Soft	Everything is New
Organization/Structure/Form	Chaos/Decomposition/Etheric	All is Possible/More

◊ When and where do I allow my individual aspects (Masculine, Feminine, and Inner Child) to express themselves which is unique unto them?

◊ When and where do I not?

◊ Does any aspect have a grievance with themselves or with another aspect of yourself?
    Masculine:
    Feminine:
    Child:

◊   What does each aspect honor and respect about themselves and one
    another?
        Masculine:
        Feminine:
        Child:

◊   What are they grateful for within themselves and about each aspect?
        Masculine:
        Feminine:
        Child:

The Forgiveness & Peace Elevation Protocol

The Elevation Code Protocols are designed to make it easier and simpler to utilize the Elevation Codes of The Diamond Co-Creative System®.
Two of the single Diamond Co-Creation Codes are combined within each
of the Elevation Codes; each Elevation Code is 10-fold the potency and
effectiveness of a single Code.

The name of the Protocol and the Elevation Codes reveal what their
purpose is and how they can help you. As you get to know a Protocol and
the Elevation Codes it uses, you can simply activate the Code, and it will
do its magic as you focus upon what your intentions are in using it and
then identify what you need and want.

You will notice that most protocols in the *CCC … Clear, Cleanse, and
Calibrate* portion of the Protocol include the Elevation Codes of Freedom,
Forgiveness, and Love. This is due to the powerful energies they provide
in the healing and completion process. Plus, the combination of the Diamond Co-Creation Code and their efficiency provide quicker results and
sustainable healing and transformation.

Let's review these three Elevation Codes:

FREEDOM

Expression

Power

Freedom Elevation Code includes the Diamond Co-Creation Codes of Expression and Power

The Expression Code works with your Karmic/Causal Energy Body, where all experiences in this lifetime and others are held. It also assists your 5th Chakra — Throat … your center of choice and voice.

You can Truly let go of the past if you're willing and allow for any past experience in this lifetime and any past life bleed throughs to be addressed, so you are no longer being affected by the past. In doing so, you can Consciously Choose to make choices that are Soul-aligned and made within present moment energetics. And you can utilize your authentic voice and allow your Soul's Essence to express through your personality Self.

The Power Code assists the Spiral Energy Body, where your family imprints and genetic and lineage encodings are held. By utilizing the Power Code, you can release imprints and encodings that are not yours, which can get in the way of your Soul's purpose and plan.

The Power Code also works with your 3rd Chakra — Solar Plexus … your center of power, Self-esteem, and will. This helps you to claim the innate power of who you Truly are and create from heart-centered power, which is tapped into your Soul's wisdom. Thus, you can feel empowered within your Conscious Choices.

Forgiveness Elevation Code includes the Diamond Co-Creation Codes of
Compassion and Foundation

The Compassion Code works with your Emotional Energy Body and the 4th Chakra — the feminine aspect of your Heart, which is where most past wounding, pain, heartache, sadness, grief, anger, resentment, regrets, and judgment of the past, yourself, and of others is held as well as the opposite — Love, joy, passion, compassion, acceptance, forgiveness, and peace.

Forgiveness is always the final step of the healing process in completing an energetic cycle that no longer serves or works for you, so this Code is important in your transformation process.

The Foundation Code that assists your Physical Body and your 1st Chakra — Root. When your Root Chakra is out of alignment, all you are doing is trying to survive, and to feel safe and secure. It also affects your finances and prosperity consciousness. Are you in lack/scarcity/not enough consciousness or prosperity/surplus/overflow consciousness?

In addition, when you hold onto unexpressed emotions, your Physical Body will begin to break down and show you what's not working through its pain, stress, illness, chronic ailments, or dis-ease. You will feel sluggish, lack energy, and even become depressed when you do not deal with your feelings.

Compassion

LOVE

Connection

Love Elevation Code includes the Diamond Co-Creation Codes of Compassion and Connection

As reviewed in the previous Elevation Code, the Compassion Co-Creation Code works with your Emotional Energy Body and your 4th Chakra — Heart (feminine). This is where the shift to Love (free of conditions), joy, passion, acceptance, and compassion can be ignited, as well as, truly feeling forgiveness and peace.

The Connection Code assists your Celestial Energy Body to make you irresistible and easily attract what's in your Highest Order and Infinite Diamond Potential.

It also works with your 7th Chakra — Crown Chakra … your command center and the connection to yourself, to your Soul, and to the Universe. Your Crown Chakra provides direct access to Universal Source energy, so it's important to keep it clear and functioning in an optimal way, so you can create, operate, and stabilize within the 5th Dimension.

The *EEE … Energize, Elevate, and Evolve* portion of the Forgiveness & Peace Protocol include the Love, Joy, Peace, Trust, and Harmony Elevation Codes. You will learn more about each of these Elevation Codes as we move through the chapters. Suffice to say, their names let you know the energetics they bring to you, especially around creating Peace and Forgiveness within.

The Forgiveness & Peace Protocol Features
The Elevation Codes of Forgiveness & Peace

We have reviewed the Forgiveness Elevation Code earlier in this chapter, so let's go to the Peace Elevation Code and how it can assist you.

Peace Elevation Code includes the Diamond Co-Creation Codes of Foundation and Grace (with the Gold Band)

The Foundation Code that assists your Physical Body and your 1st Chakra — Root. When your Root Chakra is out of alignment, you focus upon surviving, safety, and security; you let your fears 'run' you rather than the energy of Love and knowing you are always taken care of. It helps you address deep-seated fears and traumas from this lifetime and others.

The Root Chakra also affects the way you think and feel about money which determines if you are in lack or prosperity consciousness. Many times, these can be rooted in your family belief systems which you may have taken on as your own but in reality are not; you must decide what is True for you. The Foundation Code assists you to shift from survival to thrival, and from scarcity to prosperity.

In addition, when you have stagnant emotions, they will continue to build up within your Physical Body until you address them. Your Body will begin to break down to show you what's not working through physical pain, stress, illness, chronic conditions, or dis-ease. Thus, working with the Foundation Code can help heal your Physical Body, as it alerts you to the emotional release work that needs to be done.

The book, *The Secret Language of Your Body*, by Inna Segal, can reveal the meta (spiritual)-physical reasons as to why your Physical Body is showing you what needs to be addressed and energetically healed.

The Grace Code with the Gold Band works with your 11th Chakra. The 11th Chakra is below your 12th and the pathway to the Soul which allows you to embody more of your Soul's energies within your human Physical Body. The 11th is also a gateway to acquire advanced spiritual skills that you have yet to discover.

The Gold energetics provide Master Healer vibrations plus it has alchemical properties. The 11th Chakra is a transcendent alchemical energy too which helps you to "turn water into wine" so to speak.

GRACE ...
Generating Radiant Actions Creating Eternity

Grace can assist you with the process of Forgiveness and creating a sense of peace within you and around you. Eternity energies are Universal Infinite energies which can create Soul-aligned Possibilities and SOUL-utions, even when you can't imagine what they would be. Allow Grace to be a guiding power to what's possible!

The *EEE ... Energize, Elevate, and Evolve* portion of the Protocol includes the Elevation Codes of Love, Joy, Peace, Trust, and Harmony. Once you have forgiven yourself, others, or a situation, you can open your heart up and fill it with Love and joy. You begin to trust and embody that "ALL is Well" and all is in your Highest Order which leads you to find harmony and peace within you and your life.

You will find a set of all of the Elevation Codes in the appendix and you can also download full-size colored versions at: https://link.cocreateyoursuccess.com/eiyabookresourcehub.

Utilize the instructions in Chapter Six on how to use a Protocol and activate the following Protocol.

The Forgiveness & Peace Protocol
(see next page)

The Forgiveness & Peace Protocol

The Elevation Codes	The Diamond Co-Creation Codes	Code's (S) Spiritual #	Code's (M) Mental #	Code's (P) Projection #	Purposes
CCC					The Past & The Old
Freedom	Expression & Power	8	9	8	Release, Clear, Cleanse, Transmute & Calibrate
Forgiveness	Compassion & Foundation	9	3	3	Release, Clear, Cleanse, Transmute & Calibrate
Love	Compassion & Connection	3	9	3	Release, Clear, Cleanse, Transmute & Calibrate
Peace	Foundation & Grace (Gold)	11	11	22	Release, Clear, Cleanse, Transmute & Calibrate
EEE					5D — 5th Dimension
Love	Compassion & Connection	3	9	3	Energize, Elevate & Evolve into the 5D
Joy	Compassion & Anchor	7	8	6	Energize, Elevate & Evolve into the 5D
Peace	Foundation & Grace (Gold)	11	11	22	Energize, Elevate & Evolve into the 5D
Trust	Receive & Manifest	6	4	1	Energize, Elevate & Evolve into the 5D
Harmony	Receive & Wisdom	3	8	11	Energize, Elevate & Evolve into the 5D

The below is recommended verbiage only. If you are guided to change it for you, do so. The Codes 'know' exactly what you need and want.

CCC: (Name of Elevation Codes) Activate, Activate, Activate, Clear, Cleanse and Calibrate, Calibrate, Calibrate, 44 Times Divine Source Speed at the 44th Power to Purify, Purify, Purify, my Chakras and Energy Bodies to allow forgiveness of myself, others, and _____ situation and clear any incongruencies to create peace within and around me, so I move into the 5th Dimension.

Violet Flame … Transmute, Transmute, Transmute, 33 Times Divine Source Speed at the 33rd Power.

EEE: (Name of Elevation Codes) Energize, Energize, Energize, Elevate, Elevate, Elevate, Evolve, Evolve, Evolve, 44 Times Divine Source Speed at the 44th Power & saturate every cell of my Being to expand into MORE Pure Love and Peace within my heart-centered power in the 5th Dimension or Beyond and to my Highest Order and Infinite Diamond Potential.

CHAPTER NINE

The 5th Dimension Elevation Principle & Code of Love

The Elevation Principle

Pure Divine Love is Infinite … it is immeasurable. It is simple, as well as complex.

Your Soul's Essence is Pure Love, as is your original Divine blueprint. As an outbreath of the Divine, you originated from Pure Love. The Sacred Geometry of Love is the construct of the Universe in which ALL, including you, is originally sourced from the Seed of Life (a part of the Flower of Life) and Metatron's Cube.

Pure Divine Love is alive and vibrant. It is the Highest frequency in the Universe which is always moving, flowing, and expanding. It is only you who puts a limitation upon it through limiting thinking, beliefs, and feelings, which are sourced from old 3rd Dimensional paradigms and patterns. We invite you to step into the integrity and Oneness of LOVE … <u>L</u>iving <u>O</u>nly (One) <u>V</u>ibrant <u>E</u>nergy.

LOVE …
<u>L</u>iving <u>O</u>nly <u>V</u>ibrant <u>E</u>nergy

As you live life, are you REAL-ly creating through the energy of Pure Love? Are you being in integrity and REAL … <u>R</u>ealized <u>E</u>nergy <u>A</u>ligned with <u>L</u>ove with yourself and others?

Let's look at what Integrity is really based upon if it is defined through Pure Love and the 5th Dimension:

I   Infinity ... accessing ALL that is
N   Nurturing ... within evolution is nurturance
T   Transformative ... ever changing
E   Energy ... always moving and flowing
G   Generating ... even MORE and ALL energy
R   Radiance ... BE-ing the radiant energy of Pure Love
I   Integrating ... assimilating Pure Love within you
T   Total ... the wholeness of you and what you are creating
Y   Yielding ... into your MORE and ALL ... Absolute (Abundant) Light & Love

With this new definition of Integrity, we ask you to consider how you create within your life:

- Are the Creator and Co-Creator parts of you aligned with Pure Divine Love?
- Are you in Integrity with what you Truly value and with your Soul's Essence and plan?

As you dive deeper into BE-ing REAL and in Integrity, you will find it easier to step into and operate from the 5th Dimension and sustain these Higher vibrations daily. Claim your Pure Divine Love!

A Message from the Council of ALL

Greetings Dear Ones,

We invite you to practice Self-Love and Self-compassion each and every moment of the day. In doing so, this gives you the freedom to step into the 5th Dimension and beyond.

This leads you back home within your heart to your original Source connection to the quantum Universal field of Infinite Love. In this, you will discover more and more Love, joy, and peace within.

Know that you are really only Pure Divine Love ... nothing else. It is the time to remember and be in integrity with your True nature.

We love you so. Blessed Be.

Gem/Crystal for the Principle: Rose Quartz

Rose Quartz provides spiritual attunement to the energy of Love and compassion. It is especially helpful with your Heart and Crown Chakras. And it is excellent for healing emotional wounds and balancing your emotions.

Rose Quartz can bring calmness and clarity to your emotions and restores the mind to harmony after chaotic or crisis situations. It promotes receptivity to Love and beauty, and it enlivens your imagination.

Vibrates to the #7: introspection, inner work, spiritual, mystical, and wisdom.

The Universal Law of Compassion

What if today was your loved one's last day here on earth, or for that matter, your last day? How would you treat yourself or another different-ly? Would you be Loving and compassionate with yourself and others? Would you let go and free yourself from past pains, traumas, fears, worries, and judgments?

Would any of the past really matter? How would your consciousness shift if you approach life, who you are, and others with the Universal Law of Compassion as your guiding principle?

Within the consciousness of compassion, Love is free of conditions; there is no judgment and there is acceptance of one's True nature which, of course, is Divine Love. Compassion does not see the past it does not see race or color, it does not see rich or poor, and it does not see better than or less than.

Compassion allows you to be in a vibration that releases the Light of wisdom into a field of knowledge which can enrich one's life and the world. Compassion assists in creating a Unified field of Love. It flows through your heart as you connect with the Divine and your True Self … the Divinity of your Soul's Essence. This is your Diamond brilliance … the Divine-cell consciousness of who you Truly are.

When you allow yourself to be compassionate with yourself and with others, suffering, strife, lack, and drama will cease to exist. It allows the freedom for you to be in observance and awareness of what is *really* occurring within your life; and to be free of the filters from the past, pain, and trauma.

The filters are the results of our experience. We have decided whether those experiences were positive or negative. These decisions create belief systems and patterns that affect our thoughts, words, feelings, and actions. You have heard of rose-colored glasses. Well, these filters are the glasses through which we decipher each experience we have, which may or may not be the Truth of what is Truly occurring in this present moment.

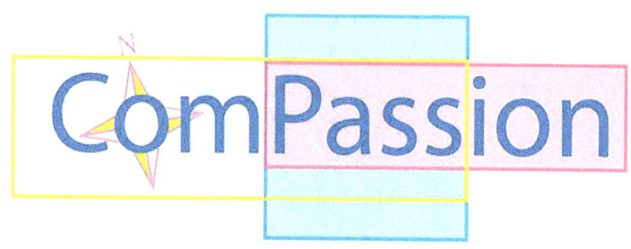

Compassion is also a tool that you can use to discern what is True for you. Within the word COMPASSION are the words COMPASS, PASSION, and PASS. When you invoke the energy of Compassion you can interpret what's being asked by a person, or if you're given an opportunity, or find yourself amid a challenge or situation, you're able to listen to your intuition and inner guidance. This is a feeling and 'knowing' from your heart and/or solar plexus.

Intuition is not a function of the mind but that of your Soul's wisdom. The gut feeling can be more from your mind, which can be at times skewed due to fear or your attachment to really wanting something or someone, while the 'knowing' is from your Soul. This is Truly felt in your heart; it's why you may have heard the expression, "drop down into or connect to your heart and feel it."

If you find you're thinking too much, or trying to figure it out, open to *feeling into* what is True. Your intuitive knowing which is felt is the COMPASS. And you can utilize it by asking "Is [whatever you're considering] in my Highest Order and Infinite Diamond Potential?"

When you feel into it, you will feel energy that is an either low or High frequency. You have tapped into your PASSION if it energizes, inspires, or uplifts you, or simply, if it feels good. If so, then your answer is "Yes!" to the question, person, or opportunity.

However, as you feel into it if your energy wanes, and you feel drained, depleted, or again it simply doesn't feel good, then this is a PASS.

Know that if you say "No" to another person, the Universe already has SOUL-ution in place for them. Trust the process ... maybe your "No" is because someone else is to help them; it's their agreement or gift to the person, and it's not yours to do, it's theirs.

The "No" can mean passing on it entirely, or just for the present moment too, because it may not be in your Highest Order or Divine Timing. If it feels neutral, then it could be a "Yes" or "No." The suggestion is to wait and check in again later.

You are now making a Conscious Choice based on Love and Compassion.

Compassion allows the freedom of detachment. When you invite it into your life, you release the attachment that yourself, others, or a situation must show up in a particular way or have a certain result. It allows for the Divine and the Universe to help you manifest the dream that is optimal for you. Remember, you may only have one piece of the puzzle and a glimpse from your limited perspective ... the Universe sees the 'big' picture.

So, how do you invoke Compassion within your life? It's easy. Just ask the question, "What would Love do?" or ask, "What would the Divine or Jesus (the Dalai Lama, Quan Yin, or an Ascended Master) do?" The other question can be "What is my Soul-aligned action?"

Simply by asking and being open to this awareness provides a means for you to surrender the past and to relieve yourself (or others) of your own crushing expectations and interpretations of you and them. Let go and forgive yourself (or others) for past perceptions that may be wrong. Let go of what you or they did or did not do, or what you or they are or are not. It's the past, leave it in the past.

Start the day with the commitment that you will treat yourself and those around you as if it is their last day on earth. It provides a consciousness, energy, and spirit of giving to yourself and others, free of conditions and in Compassion.

It is the simple smile and the simplest, most humble gesture that heals, builds, and transforms one's life and the world to be the vibration and fullness of Divine Love. It is crucial that you begin with yourself. For if you are not compassionate with yourself, then you cannot be so with others.

And remember, "We are All One." All of your thoughts, words, actions, and feelings affect your reality. We are all energy. Our energies weave together into a beautiful tapestry of creation and reality that each of us experience within our lives and in the world.

My Compassion Exploration

◊   Where am I Compassionate with myself? Where am I not?

◊   Do I *feel into* choices? Or are they based on an automatic pilot response of 'shoulds' or programming?

◊   Where are places in my life (and business) that I can practice COM-PASSION ...
    COMPASSION:
    PASSION:
    PASS:

The Universal Laws of Detachment & Faith

Today, you have the choice of freedom. And as with most choices, it means change will occur and life as you currently know will no longer be.

Let's be in curiosity ...

- Could you allow yourself to let go of something or someone that no longer serves you to have in your life anymore, or that you no longer need or desire?
- Could you choose to let go of what once was (the past) and release the attachment to its memories, whether the memories are that of Love and/or pain?
- Could you choose to be in the present moment and utilize the past only as a reference point, i.e., as a record versus your 'story' about it?
- Could you choose not to be attached to the outcome of a present circumstance, a relationship, a project, or anything or anywhere else you have invested your energy?

Can you let go of the "What if" game? Coulda, shoulda, woulda, or only if I said or did _____, is a life that is lived in the past or in the future. If you could close your eyes and create anything or anyone you desire, would it look the same as what or whom you currently have in your life? Many would answer, "No." Then how can you change what's in your current situation? The first step is to utilize the Universal Law of Detachment.

The Universal Law of Detachment provides freedom from the past and the future. It asks you to be willing to step into the field of uncertainty, and into the unknown. There is a wisdom in the uncertainty as you are willing to step into the unknown because it opens the doors into the energy field of Infinite Possibilities.

When you're not attached as to how something, someone, or a relationship 'should' look, then there is now space for so much more to occur. In that space, there is freedom for you and others to be who they Truly are, to contribute to your life and theirs in the Highest Order, and to fulfill your Soul's plan.

There is no need to control yourself, others, and outcomes, for you to create what you desire. By letting go, so much more can be manifested beyond your wildest dreams. Your results and SOUL-utions for any problems within life, situations, and relationships are much more creative, flowing, and expansive if you are detached. Detachment is a 5th Dimension core energetic.

Energy is constrictive when you have a need to push or force the solution or result *you* deem necessary. You operate within your limited scope when you impose your views and your will to manifest what you desire. If you simply surrender, you will experience a greater scheme of probabilities within your life. If you trust and have the willingness and faith to step into the unknown, SOUL-utions can occur spontaneously with ease and grace, even amid any confusion, chaos, disorder, or destruction.

However, most have the urge and need to control themselves, others, and situations in order to feel safe and secure thus producing an attachment to the outcome. Know that you are safer by letting go than by hanging on to what you think you know. Hanging on to what you think it 'should' look like actually limits the energy and the possibilities.

The other reasons for wanting to control involves the need to be right, to prove yourself, to be acknowledged or validated by someone or something outside of yourself. These needs, again, demand the attachment that people or things must be a certain way for you to feel safe and secure.

But safety and security are an inside job, not an outside one. You cannot achieve safety and security through your relationships, people, job, money, things, or even fulfilling your Soul's Purpose. Your Soul's plan is only achieved and felt in your connection within yourself and with God, Higher Power, Divine Source, or however you define this for yourself.

Some feel if you are detached, you don't or won't care, or you'll be perceived as someone who doesn't care or Love someone or something. There is the confusion that Love must 'show up' as energies of attachment and an enmeshment with someone or something for it to be real and true. This isn't True Love; it's a form of codependency.

Within the energy of attachment, there is a checklist as to what Love equals, how it must show up, and how someone must demonstrate it. This attachment doesn't allow for freedom of expression, or for the freedom of one's heart to express how it feels. Or for the possibilities of what can occur when we authentically accept the true energies of Love within the relationship.

What the Law of Detachment teaches you is that, as you step into the field of all possibilities and surrender your need to control, it allows you to remain open to the Infinity of choices. Life, full of its various kinds of creations, situations, and people, can be embraced as an adventure, an excitement, and an enthusiasm to experience it as fulfilling, magical, mysterious, and joyous. The unknown becomes a place that is no longer scary, but one of Love (Living Only Vibrant Energy), freedom, and possibilities.

The Universal Law of Faith

To support you as you embrace detachment as a way of BE-ing is the Universal Law of Faith. The Law of Faith is founded upon recognizing there is much more that we can see, taste, or feel. It is the acceptance and knowingness that there's much more beyond our limited views. Faith helps us understand that we only see pieces of the puzzle, not the whole puzzle in which we are a part of the All and are connected to Universal Love and wisdom.

We understand this when we let go and acknowledge our awareness of the miracles occurring around us and within our lives all the time. It happens when we are open to the possibilities and to receiving our Highest Order.

As we experience synchronicities within our lives, we may see them as miracles. Examples of synchronicities are … suddenly having a person who you've been thinking about calling you, or you meet someone who can help you manifest something that you've put your attention upon. Or perhaps a book falls off the shelf which answers questions you may have. Or you go to a grocery store because you listened to your intuition to go at that moment, and you meet your Beloved; the relationship you've been putting out to the Universe that you have wanted to manifest.

How we arrive at this place of recognition and trust is through the energy of Faith.

FAITH ...
Feeling Abundance In The Highest

It is understanding and knowing the connection within you, with your Soul's Essence, and with the wisdom of the Universe that provides the path to fulfill the Highest Order for yourself. Letting go of the attachments (and your egoic will, the small personality validated by others, the need to be right, safe, or secure) paves a clear path for you to reach your ultimate objectives and creations.

By listening within and through your connection with the Universe, trusting your intuition, and discerning what is in your Highest Order, Faith will flourish. You're not looking to the outside for validation, you're not letting the past dictate your decisions, and most importantly, you're not attached to your outcomes.

You realize you have the choice to play in the field of Infinite Possibilities and the unknown, when you are willing and have Faith to release the maze of the past and your attachments. You have the freedom to Consciously Choose to create your life. And, you have the power to do so at every moment!

A Tool to Assess Your Co-Dependency

A tool that you can utilize to help you explore Love and the practice of these Universal Laws is our FREE Co-Dependency Survey. This helps you to see and understand what conditioning and programming may be 'running' you and how co-dependency takes you out of BE-ing in integrity with yourself, and from BE-coming more and more Loving, compassionate, accepting, joyous, and detached from certain outcomes.

If you've taken it before, take the time to do it again to assess the shifts you have made. Give yourself 20-30 minutes to take the survey as it is very thorough, and you will receive a comprehensive report based on your answers that you can review. Go to:

https://link.cocreateyoursuccess.com/
eiyabookcodependencysurvey/

My Attachment Exploration

◊   What or with whom am I attached?

◊   Where is the fear within me that creates this attachment? Remember to ask your Inner Masculine, Feminine, and Child why they might be holding attachment and where is it sourced from?

◊   Do I feel I practice Faith daily?

◊   Are there times that my Faith wanes and why?

◊   As I look at each component of Integrity, what do I want and need to address, so I can create from the energy of Pure Love and be in Integrity with myself?

I   Infinity … accessing ALL that is:
N   Nurturing … within evolution is nurturance:
T   Transformative … ever changing:
E   Energy … always moving and flowing:
G   Generating … even MORE and ALL energy:
R   Radiance … BE-ing the radiant energy of Pure Divine Love:
I   Integrating … assimilating Pure Love within you:
T   Total … the wholeness of you and what you are creating:
Y   Yielding … into your MORE and ALL … Absolute (Abundant) Light & Love:

◊   What am I committed to … my Pure Love or Fear?

The Love Elevation Protocol

As we reviewed in the previous chapter, most protocols in the *CCC … Clear, Cleanse, and Calibrate* portion of the Protocol include the Elevation Codes of Freedom, Forgiveness, and Love. This is due to the powerful energies they provide in the healing and completion process. Plus, the combination of the Diamond Co-Creation Codes and their efficiency provide quicker results and sustainable healing and transformation.

Go to the Forgiveness & Peace chapter to further review the Freedom, Forgiveness, and Love Elevation Codes.

Included within the *CCC* portion of the Love Elevation Code Protocol is the Elevation Code of Trust. Let us review it as Trust is an important component in allowing acceptance, compassion, and Love within you and your life.

Receive   Manifest

Trust Elevation Code includes the Diamond Co-Creation Codes of Receive and Manifest

Both Diamond Co-Creation Codes work with your Third Eye — 6th Chakra, but they have different qualities and purposes. They also assist in balancing the Third Eye with the vibrations of the Masculine and the Feminine. Think of it like the right/left hemispheres of the brain which have different functions.

The Receive Code works with your Third Eye's feminine aspect … your center of intuition, inspiration, and vision. Your Feminine is the feeler, the gather, and the one who 'downloads' inspiration and ideas. The more you listen to her and Trust her, the more confident and aligned you will be to Love and to your Soul's wisdom.

Receive also assists your Gravitational Energy Body, which attracts and repels energies, people, situations, and opportunities. It depends upon your other Energy Bodies to stay in alignment for it to attract what you Truly desire, and it will repel what you no longer need, such as lessons you've already learned, people who would take you off track, and distractions that do not serve you.

If your other Energy Bodies are (or go) out of alignment with Love and what's in your Highest Order, the Gravitational Body will be out of alignment; it will then attract the lessons, people, and situations you need to learn, heal, grow, and expand from. Because of this, it sometimes feels like you are not attracting what you wanted or intended, but it is what you need to evolve into your fullest Potential.

When your Gravitational Body is out of alignment, it also repels the opportunities and people that you may be seeking because on some level you are not a vibrational match. The clue is that your results are not what you Truly want or falls short of what you envisioned.

The key is to evaluate your Chakra(s) to determine where there are energetic blocks and misalignments that are impacting your Energy Bodies. When you clear, cleanse, and calibrate your Chakra(s) that are affecting your Energy Bodies, then you can realign and repattern their energetics to become a vibrational match to what you desire. Thus, this allows the Energy Bodies to come back into alignment with your fullest Potential and so does your Gravitational Body.

The Manifest Code assists the Masculine aspect of your Third Eye — 6th Chakra. This is the center of your beliefs, discernment, and trust. Remember, as you discern what's True for you, you will trust yourself more. Discernment is not judgment; it is neutral in its observations, perceptions, feelings, thoughts, and beliefs.

Manifest works with your Mental Energy Body which creates your thoughts, beliefs, and perceptions. These create patterns and affect your neuropathways and outcomes. Change your thoughts, change your results!

The Love Protocol Features
The Elevation Code of Love

LOVE

Compassion   *Connection*

Love Elevation Code includes the Diamond Co-Creation Codes of Compassion and Connection

We reviewed each Diamond Co-Creation Code — Compassion and Connection of the Love Elevation Code in the previous chapter.

The Love Elevation Code can help transmute the past, pain, trauma, and any woundedness to Love (free of conditions), joy, acceptance, compassion, as well as truly feeling forgiveness and peace within your Heart Chakra. It can help ignite passion and desire within your Heart as you allow your Crown to open and receive Universal Source energy and your Soul's Essence and wisdom to guide you.

As the Compassion and Connection Diamond Co-Creation Codes work with your Emotional and Celestial Energy Bodies, and your Heart and Crown Chakras, they help you tap back into the Divine Love of who you Truly are. This occurs as you connect to and practice more and more Self-Love and Self-compassion.

Thus, creating space and taking time for Self-care and a daily spiritual practice to bridge the physical and the spiritual is essential. In doing so, you create even more alignment to your ALL … <u>A</u>bsolute (<u>A</u>bundant) <u>L</u>ight & <u>L</u>ove and continue your evolution of stabilizing in the 5th Dimension.

As you activate the Elevation Code of Love, you will find it easier and easier to determine when you're aligned with Pure Divine Love, and when you are out of alignment. And, activating any of the other Elevation Code(s) daily helps you to be in Integrity with yourself and with creating through Pure Divine Love.

The *EEE ... Energize, Elevate, and Evolve* portion of the Love Protocol includes the Love, Joy, Trust, Prosperity, and Thrive Elevation Codes. You will learn more about each of Joy, Prosperity, and Thrive Elevation Codes as you progress to later chapters.

Remember, their names let you know the energetics, so you can see why they are included ... who doesn't want to Trust that they can Thrive in Love, Joy, and Prosperity!?!

The Love Protocol will assist you to do BE-come more Pure Divine Love and your ALL ... <u>A</u>bundant <u>L</u>ight & <u>L</u>ove. It is suggested that you go through the Protocol at least 2-3 times a week.

Activate the Love Elevation Code daily and utilize the Love Protocol anytime you feel the need to raise your vibrations, to heal and transform any blocks to receiving and giving Love, and to boost your frequencies to embody Pure Divine Love.

Go to Chapter Six if you need a refresher on how to activate and utilize a Protocol.

The Love **Protocol**

(see next page)

The Love Protocol

The Elevation Codes	The Diamond Co-Creation Codes	Code's (S) Spiritual #	Code's (M) Mental #	Code's (P) Projection #	Purposes
CCC					The Past & The Old
Freedom	Expression & Power	8	9	8	Release, Clear, Cleanse, Transmute & Calibrate
Forgiveness	Compassion & Foundation	9	3	3	Release, Clear, Cleanse, Transmute & Calibrate
Love	Compassion & Connection	3	9	3	Release, Clear, Cleanse, Transmute & Calibrate
Trust	Receive & Manifest	6	4	1	Release, Clear, Cleanse, Transmute & Calibrate
EEE					5D – 5th Dimension
Love	Compassion & Connection	3	9	3	Energize, Elevate & Evolve into the 5D
Joy	Compassion & Anchor	7	8	6	Energize, Elevate & Evolve into the 5D
Trust	Receive & Manifest	6	4	1	Energize, Elevate & Evolve into the 5D
Prosperity	Connection & Anchor	4	1	5	Energize, Elevate & Evolve into the 5D
Thrive	Foundation & Creation	6	8	5	Energize, Elevate & Evolve into the 5D

The below is recommended verbiage only. If you are guided to change it for you, then trust it. The Codes 'know' exactly what you need and want.

CCC: (Name of Elevation Codes) Activate, Activate, Activate, Clear, Cleanse, and Calibrate, Calibrate, Calibrate, 44 Times Divine Source Speed at the 44th Power to Purify, Purify, Purify, my Chakras and Energy Bodies, any blocks to Self-Love and Self-compassion within the 5th Dimension or Beyond and to my Highest Order and Infinite Diamond Potential.

Violet Flame ... Transmute, Transmute, Transmute, 33 Times Divine Source Speed at the 33rd Power.

EEE: (Name of Elevation Codes) Energize, Energize, Energize, Elevate, Elevate, Elevate, Evolve, Evolve, Evolve 44 Times Divine Source Speed at the 44th Power and saturate every cell of my Being to expand into MORE of my heart-centered power with the freedom to give and receive Pure Divine Love and compassion in equal measure for myself and others within the 5th Dimension or Beyond and in my Highest Order and Infinite Diamond Potential.

CHAPTER TEN

The 5ᵗʰ Dimension Elevation Principle & Code of Joy

The Elevation Principle

In the 5th Dimension you learn, grow, heal, transform, and expand through JOY … Journey Onward Yielding.

JOY …
Journey Onward Yielding

You are on a *journey*. The journey of life, the journey of your Soul, and the journey of your evolution.

Onward is the energy of movement. You never really go backwards, even though at times it seems like it. Energy moves forward which helps you to *yield* into what your journey and Soul's plan wants for you.

Joy can assist you to *yield* into what's possible, what's next, and what wants to come forth. *Yielding* into letting go, surrendering, and allowing. *Yielding* into the connection with your Soul's Essence. *Yielding* into Infinite Possibilities and SOUL-utions. *Yielding* into your MORE, Highest Order, and Infinite Diamond Potential!

In the 3rd Dimension, you learn through pain, suffering, and/or struggle, but in the 5th Dimension you can Consciously Choose to learn through Joy. Pain is a sign that some sort of distortion of what's really True (such as outdated conditioning, programming, and interpretation of experiences) is at the core of an issue.

When you embrace the Divine and your Divinity, you can reclaim the trust in yourself and the Universe. You will allow Joy to guide you, rather than be guided by your pain, or by the need to fix a problem or solve a crisis.

It is a matter of breaking the cycle and disrupting the patterns that you must suffer, struggle, and sacrifice in order to get through challenges and to grow. In the 3rd Dimension, you were taught that you have to *overcome* obstacles, rather than *flow* through them. Consciously Choose to step out of the old 3D model and step into the new 5D paradigm.

To co-create what you REAL-ly want, it is essential to focus upon an expanded vibrational energy and elevated consciousness. If you focus on what's not, then you're 'vibing' out constrictive energy. However, if you focus on what *feels* in alignment of what works and what you like, then the doorway opens into the ALL … <u>A</u>bsolute (<u>A</u>bundant) <u>L</u>ight & <u>L</u>ove.

Today, invite in Joy. Think about a time when you felt happy, or about someone or something that makes you feel joy i.e., a loved one, children playing, gazing into the eyes of your pet who loves you, a fun trip, the beach, nature, or anything that puts a smile on your face and makes you feel uplifted and inspired. Breathe it in and recall how it feels. Where do you feel it in your Physical Body?

Bring it into your heart and allow the feeling and the warmth of Joy's vibration infuse within your Charkas and spread throughout your Energy Bodies — Physical, Emotional, Mental, and Spiritual.

Joy emanates from your Soul's Essence and comes from within without the need for outside influence. Joy is a feeling, a vibration, and a Consciousness that you can evoke and access at any time and bring into any situation, even when it's frustrating or challenging. Whereas happiness derives from what is going on outside of you; it is conditional and circumstantial.

Joy is how you can vibrationally shift a lower and restrictive energy, such as your fear, doubt, worry, anger, sadness, disappointment, or upset into a Higher and more expansive frequency and energy.

Remember, it becomes a Conscious Choice as to what kind of energy you want to experience, feel, live into, and co-create within.

A Message from the Council of ALL

Greetings Dear Ones,
We invite you to give yourself permission to live in Joy. You are not on the earth to suffer or to be in pain although this might seem contrary to

what you have experienced. This is sourced from your 3rd Dimensional way of experiencing life and how you think and believe growth should occur.

We are here to let you know that you can still learn and grow through Joy — your struggle no longer needs to be part of your formula. Consciously Choose the paradigm of Joy to create and co-create within ... choose to be present in the vibration of Joy as you go throughout your day even if it is a difficult day.

Observe when you are in Joy and observe when you are not. Call upon us to help lift you into Joy. Radiate Joy out into the world and be the beacon of the ALL — Abundant Light and Love.

We love you so. Blessed Be.

Gem/Crystal for the Principle: Sapphire

Sapphire helps to bring Joy and peace of mind by ridding yourself of unwanted thoughts and opening your mind to beauty and intuition. It brings in lightness and Joy. It assists you to focus upon and radiate energy (even without your conscious initiation).

It is known as a "stone of prosperity," which sustains the gifts of life and eliminates frustration as you fulfill your dreams and desires. Sapphire attracts the energy of cooperation at the cellular level.

Vibrates to #2: partnership, balance, unity, harmony, and being of service.

The Universal Law of Perfection

The Universal Law of Perfection relates to the absolute perfection of your journey and the process of your unfolding. From a transcendental (spiritual) perspective, everyone and everything is already perfect. From a conventional viewpoint, perfection doesn't exist. Because what is perfection, really?

Doing the best you can with what you know is another way of looking at perfection. It also allows you to be in Joy no matter what. In that, you are always yielding into more of your Diamond brilliance and excellence. You are allowing for more Light and Love into your BE-ingness as you Love and accept yourself in any given moment, despite any particular outcome.

As you understand there is a 'bigger' picture of YOU and your Divine unfoldment, you can let go of the *need* to be perfect and to *prove* you are perfect. You can let go of demanding that you and things must be perfect. You can let go of others being perfect.

You can claim Joy in the moment. You can accept and be present with what is, is. This opens the pathway for you to become more Loving, compassionate, giving, kinder, and gentler with yourself and with others. This opens the allowance of Divine Flow … a 5th Dimension quality and vibration.

You can Consciously Choose Joy in the perfection of who you are NOW!

The Universal Law of Divine Flow

The Universal Law of Divine Flow is about living in the present moment, centering yourself in Love, and being in service to others. You stay in the Flow of your Soul's Essence and Divine guidance moment by moment.

FLOW ...
Freely Living in your Own Wisdom

By 'owning' your wisdom and reflecting Love and allowance, there is a 5th Dimensional Flow in how you think, feel, speak, and do. With Divine Flow you are aligned and connected to your Soul and the Universe. As you continue to allow and trust the Flow, you will deepen and strengthen your connection with the Divine and your Divinity. You will be able to stay in energetic integrity and gain emotional and spiritual maturity.

Flow is the movement of energy, or any element, such as air, water, love, joy, money, etc. Flow is continuous whether it is freely Flowing, or if it is limited or blocked. There's always some sort of movement even when you feel stuck because at least you'll recognize that it's not Flowing or Flowing in the way you would like it to be.

And the energy is either an Etheric, Radiant, or Vibrant Flow. As you acknowledge whether you are in an open or restricted Flow, you can identify the type of Flow and its intention and purpose. Then, you will come to understand and feel the action of the Flow.

The process of Etheric, Radiant, and Vibrant Flow is not necessarily linear. It occurs on multi-dimensional levels in all time, space, and dimensions within all parts of your BE-ing and Soul's Essence.

Etheric Flow comes to you as imagination, concepts, ideas, innovations, and inspirations for things such as a book, a project, teachings, or parts of your life, including your growth, spirituality, health, money, relationships, career or business, co-creations, and much more. Etheric Flow is the energy of Eternity, which is Infinite Possibilities, probabilities, SOUL-utions.

The Etheric is that which is above you, so to speak, in the ethers, in your superconscious and Soul, and within the Universe waiting to be 'downloaded' into your consciousness and expressed through your personality Self. The Etheric Flow 'downloads' into your mind and heart and becomes Radiant Flow.

However, depending on what is occurring vibrationally within your cellular memory, your energetic patterns, your Chakras, and your Energy Bodies, especially your Physical, Emotional, Mental, and Spiritual Energy Bodies, the Etheric Flow is affected in how it is assimilated and integrated. Does it Flow in a free and expansive manner, or is it energetically limited or blocked in some way?

Radiant Flow helps identify the various types of energy. It is the energy downloaded and infused from the Etheric Flow. Radiant Flow energy enters the heart and mind, integrating into the human being who stands within it. The Radiant Flow is affected by the energetics you currently hold which are the vibrations of your patterns, thoughts, feelings, beliefs, imprints, and encodings at the cellular level. These are held within your Chakras, Energy Bodies, and cellular memory.

Is the Etheric Flow easily assimilated through a Radiant Flow of energy? Are you vibrationally aligned with it, or are there incongruent energies which create stress, blocks, and difficulty in aligning with the Etheric downloads and your Highest Order and Infinite Diamond Potential?

So, what Radiant Flow of energy are you standing in ... Love, joy, compassion, thrival, passion, purpose, OR fear, survival, sadness, judgment, doubt, worry, etc.? What are you Radiating from your cellular memory, your energetic patterns, your Chakras, and your Energy Bodies, then 'vibing out' to others and to the Universe? What is congruent or incongruent with your intentions?

Radiant Flow helps you to understand the intention and purpose of the energy showing up within you and around you. It provides you with useful data so you can create the changes required if your Radiant Flow is incongruent with what you want and does not allow for the manifestations you desire.

But, if the Radiant Flow is congruent with your desires, it assists you to build momentum as the Etheric and Radiant Energy Flow freely through you. It is in vibrational alignment with your desires and intentions.

It is the 'who' you are vibrationally BE-ing within your energetic makeup and design, and within your intentions and vision. This is the BE-ing part of the co-creative process of manifestation. It is how and what you think, feel, believe, and know.

Vibrant Flow is the action you take (consciously or unconsciously) in co-creating the Radiant Flow to become a physical manifestation on the planet. The manifestation may or may not be what you desire because of who and what you are 'vibing' out. The Vibrant Flow is who and what you 'vibe' out to others and to the Universe.

To create the results you want, you must BE in vibrational alignment to the Etheric Flow and Radiant Flow of the energy within you. If it's not what you want, then you must address and change it on a vibrational energetic level. This means to energetically heal and complete the past, the old patterns, conditioning, programming, and the 3rd Dimension paradigm you may be co-creating within, especially if they are not giving you the outcomes you desire.

The Vibrant Flow is what you DO to develop, implement, and produce in physical form and manifestations of your Radiant Flow. This is the DO-ing part of the co-creative process of manifestation and the projection out into the world. It is the result and outcome of your BE-ingness.

My Joy Exploration

◊   What and who brings me Joy?

◊   How do I step out of Joy?

◊   How do I let a person or situation take me out of my Joy?

◊   Do I give myself permission to live in Joy, or do I need to have problems, crisis, and drama to solve in my life to feel alive?

◊   What do I notice about the different aspects of my Flow?

◊   Am I in Flow? If not, what blockages are restricting my Flow?

◊ Am I willing to allow Flow?

◊ Am I committed to living in Joy and Flow?

The Joy Elevation Protocol

As with other Protocols, the *CCC … Clear, Cleanse, and Calibrate* portion of the Protocol include the Elevation Codes of Freedom, Forgiveness, and Love. With this Protocol, we added the Joy Elevation Code to the *CCC* portion of the Protocol. Each Elevation Code helps you to heal any pain of the past, the suffering and the struggle, so you can Consciously Choose Joy, despite any challenge or current circumstance and conditions. You choose to learn and grow through Joy rather than in pain, suffering, or struggle.

In the *EEE … Energize, Elevate, and Evolve* portion of the Protocol, we included Love, Joy, Freedom, and added the Passion and Trust Elevation Codes. This activates your Soul's passion and guides you into being more passionate within your life, relationships, and vocation. It helps build trust with the Universe and with yourself as you have more confidence and belief in yourself.

Let's review how the Passion Elevation Code can assist you …

Passion Elevation Code includes the Diamond Co-Creation Codes of Creation and Power

The Creation Code works with your Sacral Chakra — 2nd Chakra which is your center of creativity, health and well-being, and the Divine Feminine to help create Sacred Union with the Divine Masculine. When your Sacral Chakra is in alignment you feel vibrant and full of vitality. You can attain optimal health and well-being.

You allow the Flow of Divine creativity fueled by your Soul's energies and wisdom to guide you and be creative beyond your imagination. You learn to follow the energies as to what wants to be created. You trust the co-creative process of the dance and weave between your Masculine and Feminine so you can create the life you want and fulfill your desires, purpose, and passion.

The Creation Code also assists the Astral Energy Body that protects your Physical Body from perceived threats to keep you safe. If you feel fearful or not yourself, check your Astral Body and see if it is being compromised and alerting you that something is off.

We reviewed the Power Code in a prior chapter. As a reminder, it helps your Power center — 3rd Chakra to feel empowered and aligned with heart-centered power. It helps you to clear any fears of being in your power or low Self-esteem. In addition, it helps to transform any old Lineage and Genetic encodings within your Spiral Energy Body, as well as other familial imprints that no longer serve you in this lifetime.

The Joy Protocol Features
The Elevation Code of Joy

Joy Elevation Code includes the Diamond Co-Creation Codes of Compassion and Anchor

The Compassion Code works with your Emotional Energy Body and the feminine aspect of your Heart — 4th Chakra which we covered in previous chapters. As you heal the 'wounded' heart, or any 'wounded' aspect of yourself (Masculine, Feminine, or Inner Child) within your Heart, it assists the Emotional Body to feel and experience more Love, Joy, and harmony within and with others.

The Compassion Code helps to dissolve blocks and allow for the emotions … *energy in motion* to Flow within Joy … Journey Onward Yielding. As you focus on Higher frequencies and positivity, you will feel more energized, enthusiastic, and inspired. You will emanate Love and Joy within yourself and out into the world to others.

The Anchor Code on the right assists the masculine aspect of the Heart — 4th Chakra and your Spiritual Energy Body. The Spiritual Body houses your lower Chakras (1st-7th), so the Anchor Code is a quick and easy way to help your Chakras to be cleared, move into present time, and invoke the High frequency vibrations you desire.

The Anchor Code assists you to become aligned as to what your crown achievements are to pursue and manifest in this lifetime; it helps you to create your legacy. It assists you to anchor in the Highest Order and Infinite Diamond Potential within your Heart. You become heart-centered and authentic in who you are and what you came here to experience and do.

Below is the Joy Protocol and remember go to Chapter Six if you need assistance in how to use it. The Joy Protocol will assist you to experience MORE Joy and heal the energetics which are not congruent with Joy. It is suggested to do it at least 2-3 times a week.

Plus, as you activate the Elevation Code of Joy each day, you will find it easier and easier to determine when you're in alignment with Joy, and when you are out of alignment. Activating the Elevation Code(s) on a daily basis helps you to create through Joy!

The Joy Protocol
(see next page)

The Joy Protocol

The Elevation Codes	The Diamond Co-Creation Codes	Code's (S) Spiritual #	Code's (M) Mental #	Code's (P) Projection #	Purposes
CCC					The Past & The Old
Freedom	Expression & Power	8	9	8	Release, Clear, Cleanse, Transmute & Calibrate
Forgiveness	Compassion & Foundation	9	3	3	Release, Clear, Cleanse, Transmute & Calibrate
Love	Compassion & Connection	3	9	3	Release, Clear, Cleanse, Transmute & Calibrate
Joy	Compassion & Anchor	7	8	6	Release, Clear, Cleanse, Transmute & Calibrate
EEE					5D – 5th Dimension
Love	Compassion & Connection	3	9	3	Energize, Elevate & Evolve into the 5D
Joy	Compassion & Anchor	7	8	6	Energize, Elevate & Evolve into the 5D
Freedom	Expression & Power	8	9	8	Energize, Elevate & Evolve into the 5D
Passion	Creation & Power	9	1	1	Energize, Elevate & Evolve into the 5D
Trust	Receive & Manifest	6	4	1	Energize, Elevate & Evolve into the 5D

The verbiage below is recommended only. If you are guided to change it for you, then do so. The Codes 'know' exactly what you need and want.

CCC: (Name of Elevation Codes) Activate, Activate, Activate, Clear, Cleanse, and Calibrate, Calibrate, Calibrate, 44 Times Divine Source Speed at the 44th Power to Purify, Purify, Purify, my Chakras and Energy Bodies, any blocks or restrictions to Joy and Flow in the 5th Dimension or Beyond and to my Highest Order and Infinite Diamond Potential.

Violet Flame ... Transmute, Transmute, Transmute, 33 Times Divine Source Speed at the 33rd Power.

EEE: (Name of Elevation Codes) Energize, Energize, Energize, Elevate, Elevate, Elevate, Evolve, Evolve, Evolve 44 Times Divine Source Speed at the 44th Power and saturate every cell of my Being with MORE Joy and openness to receive an abundance of Etheric, Radiant, and Vibrant Flow within myself, and in my life, health, relationships, business, money, and _____ in the 5th Dimension or Beyond and in my Highest Order and Infinite Diamond Potential.

CHAPTER ELEVEN

The 5th Dimension Elevation Principle & Code of Prosperity

The Elevation Principle

By allowing MORE flow into your life, you attract even MORE Prosperity through your radiance.

Prosperity means much more than attaining financial wealth. It is finding joy, fulfillment, and contentment of your success in any and all areas of your life, regardless of whether it is small or big. In other words, Prosperity is realized by succeeding in healthy ways, celebrating your wins along the way, and thriving in life.

The first records of the word *prosperity* come from around 1200AD. It comes from the Latin word *prosperitās*. The suffix *-ity* is used to form abstract nouns, indicating a state or condition. The verb *prosper* comes from the Latin *prosperāre*, meaning 'to make happy.' The Old French from Latin prosperus is 'favorable.' The Latin word also means 'fortunate,' and the word Prosperity does have an element of good luck.

However, to attract and attain Prosperity, it's important to elevate your consciousness onto a High frequency of Prosperity, rather than be in scarcity or lack ways of thinking, feeling, and believing. Your perception requires a shift from not enough to plenty and surplus, with the flow of abundance coming your way versus having to chase after it.

This applies to any aspect within your life: Love, joy, relationships, energy, health and vitality, money, opportunities, clients, etc. To create

Prosperity consciousness, you must make a Conscious Choice to think, feel, and believe in abundant ways to allow it to flow.

Thus, your Radiant energy of abundance and Prosperity 'vibes' out to the world. It successfully attracts what you Truly desire. It is also being able to discern when you're 'off track' and realizing what or whom is a misalignment and blocking your fullest Potential and Highest Order.

Plus, if you accept and know in your heart that you are *already* successful in what you have created, manifested, and achieved thus far in your life, you become more prosperous. This helps you release "I'm not good enough," or "I didn't do enough," which perpetuates the proving, over-compensating, over-responsibility, over-giving, and over-doing, and even over-thinking patterning, conditioning, and programming.

And you can always ask for MORE! This doesn't take away from what you have received. The Universe is Infinite, so asking for more does not negate the importance and gratitude of what you have already received.

Being in gratitude is a key element in the flow of Prosperity. Be grateful for what you have, rather than complain about what you don't have, or what is not here yet. Eventually, you will realize that you can ask for ALL. This takes you into the 5th Dimension and beyond, as you step into the continuum of evolution. In the ALL, you *are* the Creator steeped in Abundant Light and Love!

A Message from the Council of ALL

Greetings Dear Ones,

We invite you to give yourself permission to be in the flow of Prosperity. Consciously Choose the paradigm of success and joy to create and co-create within, so you can be present with the vibration of plenty, surplus, and overflow.

Allow yourself to elevate into the 5th Dimension of Prosperity consciousness. Continue to expand into the ALL of the Infinite Universe and know this is available to you.

It is up to you to make a Conscious Choice to ask us, focus upon what's possible, give gratitude, and be open to receiving ALL that we desire to give you.

For you are worthy of having it ALL in life and BE-ing Abundant Light and Love!

We love you so. Blessed Be.

Gem/Crystal for the Principle: Citrine

Citrine is most often called 'the Merchant's Stone.' It supports the idea that when you find your joy, wealth and abundance will follow. It helps you to acquire wealth, as well as maintain a *state* of wealth.

It is useful for balancing yin-yang energy. Citrine activates, opens, and energizes the Solar Plexus — your Power center to create Self-confidence. It works with your Root Chakra to eliminate fear and the need to survive. It helps with mental focus, endurance, and vision.

Citrine does not hold or accumulate negative energies.

It vibrates to the #6: Love, family, home, relationships, harmony, and being of service.

The Universal Law of Success

Have you based the criteria of your success on someone else's standard, your bank account, or the types of relationships in your life? Have you felt like you've made a mistake or failed many times at what you set out to do? Have you compared your success with others? In other words, do you measure your success by the 'outside' outcomes rather than from the 'inside' state of BE-ing?

The Universal Law of Success is Truly about you and the integration of your True Self ... your Soul's Essence and the Divine energies of the Universe. It is the ability to create from an energy of synthesizing simplicity and synchronicity, which brings you LOVE ... Living Only Vibrant Energy. The simplicity is that of, less is more, because you allow the Divine to work through you.

You don't have to work hard for the money, so to speak; it's not about effort, but instead of flow. The flow is manifested through the synchronicity aspect of energies organizing and lining up within the Universe to physically accomplish something you've intended and focused upon to create.

Many perceive success from an old perspective. Success for some is evaluated by a set of one or more old paradigm criteria, i.e., what goals you've attained, how the results look, how much money you've earned or have in the bank, how many awards you've won, what you've accomplished in life, etc.

Many times, you're grinding it out and, at times, forcing something to happen. Notice when you use the phrase, "I am going to make this happen," rather than co-creating it with your Soul and the Universe.

In perceiving success through the latter criteria, the opposite of success is *failure,* a concept attached to certain results, survival, and limitations. This energy is dense and foreboding, as well as depressive and full of fearful energies like guilt, shame, anger, resentment, 'should,' separation, blame, and/or victim. Many feel they have failed based on the goals and expectations of themselves and/or others. This does not leave room for you to thrive, nor the flow of Prosperity … joy, contentment, and True fulfillment.

However, from the perspective of this Universal Law of Success, the opposite of success is simply *not yet,* not failure. Can you feel the difference in this energy? It is a continuation of looking at:

- ✦ what are my next steps guided by the Divine and my Soul?
- ✦ what is the Divine Timing and Highest Order?
- ✦ what possibly needs to be realigned within my energetics?
- ✦ what MORE is being created in the etheric, *not yet* present in the physical?

Looking at a perceived mistake or failure this way, creates a moving forward and thriving energy. *Not yet* has an understanding, belief, and faith that all is in Divine Order and Timing. It congratulates you for your accomplishments along the way, each and every step, no matter how small or how big.

Your new definition of success:

SUCCESS ...

*Self Unifying through Conscious Choice to Energize
Simplicity and Synchronicity*

It is about you Consciously co-creating through the connection you have within yourself, with your Soul's passion, purpose, and plan, and with the Universe. It is not about creating or living in the past, or from within the box of the 'old' you. The true meaning of insanity is doing the same thing, the same way, and expecting the result to be different.

Thus, the Universal Law of Vibration comes into play.

The Universal Law of Vibration

As we know, everything is energy; it has a vibration that is always moving and never rests. A vibration is composed of frequency and there are Higher and lower frequencies. The words Higher, lower, or good, bad are used here to represent the qualities of the words, not as a judgment or a better than, less than value.

Higher and good means less dense, and a more rapid, smooth pace in which the energy can easily flow. For example, Love has a vibration of expansiveness, freedom, and the frequency is fast paced. While fear is a denser vibration of constriction, bondage, and the frequency is slow, and its flow is thwarted.

The Universal Law of Vibration asks you … what are your *underlying motivations* for what you do and create? If your intentions and desires are centered around Love and 'vibed' out to be the best that you can BE and DO, to be of service, or to contribute to the greater good for All, then the vibration has a Higher frequency. There are synchronicities and orchestrations that occur *for* you. They magnetize back to the origin (YOU) the gifts of Higher frequencies.

If there are underlying fears such as lack or scarcity that are fueling your motivations (consciously or unconsciously), or even some sort of selfish reasons, then the energies drawn to you and reflected to you are vibrations of decreased frequency levels. The results are a lower frequency that is moving within both yourself and your manifestations. It will not be what you really want, and you will be most assuredly disappointed. The outcome is out of sync with your intentions, and it will fall short of what you envisioned.

You can identify this if you are energized and inspired by something you're doing, or by those that surround you; it feels aligned, and you are manifesting the type of results you want. But, if what you're doing requires a lot of *effort* and you're frustrated and upset with the results you're receiving, then the energies are showing you there is not a vibrational alignment with your desire. This gives you the opportunity to evaluate what is out of integrity and alignment within your Chakras and Energy Bodies, and with your intentions.

This does not mean you have to purge everything you are doing, or even everyone in your life. The Universe is showing you what is a vibrational match and what is not. It is also revealing your true motivating factor. If what you're doing is just focused on just making money and not being in service, or only for your gain, you will assuredly be disappointed with the lack of flow. How can you shift so you can utilize and share your zone of genius to make a difference in other people's lives, in the workplace or in your business, and in the world?

Let go of unrealistic expectations; if you expect to take a leap in revenue such as $1000 to $10,000 a month without doing the 'inner' work to match it, then you will, again, be disappointed. If you want Love, but don't feel worthy of Love or give it to others without conditions, then you will be most assuredly discouraged by the people you attract.

Be sure to look at your energy–your thoughts, words, beliefs, and feelings. Are you in a High frequency consciousness such as Prosperity consciousness, or a scarcity (not enough, not good enough, lack) consciousness?

It might be as simple as *redefining* and *refining* your desires and motivations. It could be the need to clean up the past, since you are no longer the person you once were, and your motivating factors have changed. In the 3rd Dimension, your motivations were driven by ambition and fear, while in the 5th Dimension, they are Soul-aligned and sourced through Love.

This is part of the co-creative process and life's journey. Remember, nothing stays the same … vibrationally energy is always moving so that means we are too. Plus, there is always (and in all ways) forward movement; you can't go back, except to resolve and heal what no longer is or serves you in the Highest Order.

You are always evolving, even when it doesn't look or feel like it in a given moment. Choose differently; choose your Prosperity consciousness and trust yourself and the Universe!

My Prosperity Exploration

◊   How do I define Success?

◊   What is my *not yet*?

◊   What does Prosperity mean to me?

◊   Do I live in lack, scarcity, or 'not enough' conscious and, if so, how? What are my lower frequency and 3rd Dimension thoughts, beliefs, and feelings?

◊   What could be my new 5th Dimension Prosperity thoughts, beliefs, and feelings?

◊   What does Prosperity consciousness look like and feel like for me?

◊   How am I *already* prosperous? And how can I build my trust and faith within these examples?

◊   Am I grateful for what I already have and how do I express it?

◊   Do I give myself permission to attract even MORE prosperity?

◊   Am I in Flow? If not, what vibrations are misaligned within my Flow of Prosperity?

◊   Am I committed to live in Prosperity? Will I make a Conscious Choice to do so?

The Prosperity Elevation Protocol

As a reminder, the Diamond Co-Creation Codes that combine together to create the Elevation Codes are composed of patterns of Sacred Geometry. Sacred Geometry bridges science and spirituality by bringing nature and Spirit together in all life forms.

The Diamond Co-Creation Codes are ever fluid and shifting energies, as they incorporate the Sacred Geometry of original Creation (pure nature form and Love) and spiritual consciousness. The Codes activate your consciousness to create a deeper sense of connection, understanding, Divine Truth, and co-creation.

The Elevation Codes and each of their Codes assist you in spiraling out the energies, patterns, and belief systems that are ready to be released by your intention of healing (including all that is conscious or unconscious).

They shift the energy to realign with your original Divine blueprint of Love and re-pattern your cellular memory. The Codes can also spiral back to you the energies of alignment with your True Self, intentions, desires, and Divine Will and Order. With the use of the Infinity Breath, you can experience dynamic shifts, assimilation, and integration of healings, new belief systems and paradigms, intentions, and creations.

The *CCC ... Clear, Cleanse, and Calibrate* portion of the Prosperity Protocol includes the Freedom, Forgiveness, Love, and Prosperity Elevation Codes. These offer you an opportunity to let go of the past, any perceived mistakes or failures, and your lack and scarcity consciousness, as well as your preconceived notions of success. You do so by utilizing it as a tool to release what no longer serves you, or what you desire to complete within you and with others.

Within the *EEE ... Energize, Elevate, and Evolve* portion of the Prosperity Protocol are Love, Harmony, Trust, Abundant, and Prosperity Elevation Codes. We have already covered Love and Trust in prior chapters, plus we will go into depth of Harmony and Abundant in Chapters Sixteen and Seventeen.

The Prosperity Protocol Features
The Elevation Code of Prosperity

Prosperity Elevation Code includes the Diamond Co-Creation Codes of Connection and Anchor

The Connection Code assists your Celestial Energy Body (least dense Energy Body) to make you irresistible and easily attract what (and whom) is in your Highest Order and Infinite Diamond Potential. It also works with your 7th Chakra — the Crown Chakra connecting you to you, to your Soul, and to the Universe. As you keep it open and clear, you have more direct access to Universal Source energy to help you operate and stabilize in the 5th Dimension.

The Connection Code assists you connect to the Divine Truth of you, of your Soul, and of any situation, rather than through the veil of your egoic mind truth. You may feel your Crown Chakra tingle, or energy rushing into and throughout your Body when your Crown is open and connected to the Divine and your Soul's Essence.

The Anchor Code assists the Masculine aspect of the Heart — 4th Chakra and your Spiritual Energy Body. Since the Spiritual Body houses your lower Chakras (1st–7th), Anchor can help you to keep in the vibrations of Light and Love as you fill your Chakras with High frequency energies. You are then guided by your Heart and Soul as to what to pursue and manifest in your life.

The Prosperity Elevation Code can assist you to anchor within your heart the vibrations of Prosperity consciousness, so that you think, feel, and believe in these terms, and take action accordingly. You can let go of the past experiences which support your lack and 'not enough' consciousness and choose to anchor in the Higher vibrations of abundant Prosperity!

By working and meditating with this Protocol, you will observe and/or feel it as multidimensional, assisting you on many levels and within your Chakras and Energy Bodies to realign with the True meaning of success and Prosperity. The vibrations of the Elevation Codes of Love, Prosperity, Harmony, Trust, and Abundant help you connect with abundant Prosperity within all aspects of your life.

It is suggested to do the Protocol at least 2-3 times a week. Plus, as you activate the Elevation Code of Prosperity, you will find it easier and easier to determine when you are out of alignment with Prosperity and to choose Prosperity consciousness. Activating the Elevation Code(s) on a daily basis helps you maintain these new vibrations.

You can co-create your success in a whole new way. You can claim and radiate your Prosperity consciousness and thrive with the implementation of this 5th Dimension Principle and Protocol.

The Prosperity Protocol ...
Expand My Prosperity Consciousness & Flow of Abundance
(see next page)

The Prosperity Protocol ... Expand My Prosperity Consciousness & Flow of Abundance

The Elevation Codes	The Diamond Co-Creation Codes	Code's (S) Spiritual #	Code's (M) Mental #	Code's (P) Projection #	Purposes
CCC					The Past & The Old
Freedom	Expression & Power	8	9	8	Release, Clear, Cleanse, Transmute & Calibrate
Forgiveness	Compassion & Foundation	9	3	3	Release, Clear, Cleanse, Transmute & Calibrate
Love	Compassion & Connection	3	9	3	Release, Clear, Cleanse, Transmute & Calibrate
Prosperity	Connection & Anchor	4	1	5	Release, Clear, Cleanse, Transmute & Calibrate
EEE					5D – 5th Dimension
Love	Compassion & Connection	3	9	3	Energize, Elevate & Evolve into the 5D
Harmony	Receive & Wisdom	3	8	11	Energize, Elevate & Evolve into the 5D
Trust	Receive & Manifest	6	4	1	Energize, Elevate & Evolve into the 5D
Abundant	Gratitude (Silver) & Receive	8	2	1	Energize, Elevate & Evolve into the 5D
Prosperity	Connection & Anchor	4	1	5	Energize, Elevate & Evolve into the 5D

The below is recommended verbiage. If you are guided change it for you, follow the guidance. The Codes 'know' exactly what you need and want.

CCC: (Name of Elevation Codes) Activate, Activate, Activate, Clear, Cleanse, and Calibrate, Calibrate, Calibrate, 44 Times Divine Source Speed at the 44th Power to Purify, Purify, Purify, my Chakras and Energy Bodies, so they can embody and vibrate Prosperity consciousness in all parts of my BE-ing in the 5th Dimension and to my Highest Order and Infinite Diamond Potential.

Violet Flame ... Transmute, Transmute, Transmute, 33 Times Divine Source Speed at the 33rd Power.

EEE: (Name of Elevation Codes) Energize, Energize, Energize, Elevate, Elevate, Elevate, Evolve, Evolve, Evolve 44 Times Divine Source Speed at the 44th Power and saturate abundant Prosperity in every cell of my Being so I expand within abundant Prosperity consciousness in the 5th Dimension and align with my Highest Order and Infinite Diamond Potential.

CHAPTER TWELVE

The 5th Dimension Elevation Principle of Thrive

The Elevation Principle

Thrive is a state of BE-ing, while engaged in any activity of DO-ing. It is a 5th Dimension quality of consciousness of the 'AND,' rather than 'either/or.'

Thrive is the interweaving of BE-ing and DO-ing. It is not an either/ or paradigm. As you DO, you can BE present in the moment by radiating a certain vibration; it is filling in the energetic gap through the vibrational qualities of your consciousness. The vibration of the type of consciousness you live in is your choice ... to operate within scarcity, not enough, and survival consciousness, or to choose Prosperity and thriving conscious-ness within the 5th Dimension.

There are two components of Thrive. The first is moving out of the old paradigm of survival, and into the energy of thrival. The second is a paradigm shift from either/or to AND. The 5th Dimension of Thrive opens the doorway to vigorously grow and to progress toward (or realize) a goal, despite (or because) of any current condition or circum-stance. It is a vibration directly connected to your Prosperity and wealth consciousness.

Consciousness is the quality, or state of BE-ing aware, especially of something within oneself. Most were taught and grew up with the simple need to survive. Thus, all of your BE-ing will operate from survival beliefs, thoughts, feelings, words, and actions. This need to survive leads you to thinking and feeling like you have only one choice, an either/or choice, then your state of BE-ing operates from this paradigm.

If the energetics of survival and either/or radiate throughout you, then you are operating in a lower 3rd Dimension frequency that is based on fear, rather than Love. Thrive energies create the energetics of the ability to flourish, succeed, prosper, rise, shine, grow, develop, expand, grow, bloom, and blossom into your Diamond brilliance and Infinite Potential.

To reconfigure and reset, you must identify the source of your current consciousness. For instance, if you address the vibrations of the need to survive, it is typically held in the following:

- Your Physical Body — it is inherent that the Body wants to survive and not die, so it will protect itself by whatever means necessary.
- Your Genetic Encoding — within the encoding that you inherited through your birth parents, you are predisposed to certain biological and chemical genetics.
- Your Lineage Encoding — these are energetic patterns that are passed down through your ancestral and cultural lineages.
- Your Conditioning and Programming which affects your Emotional and Mental Energy Bodies — it's what you have witnessed and been taught, what you have learned (in this lifetime and others), and what you've experienced through your own life lessons, or from others, society, and mass consciousness.

The above also applies to the consciousness of either/or. Either/or brings in the energies of sacrifice, scarcity, and separation. It does not allow you to claim your Divine birthrights and beliefs that you can have it ALL! The ALL is an expansion of your consciousness, which leads you into your ability to Thrive within in a paradigm shift of your prosperity and wealth consciousness.

And, the ALL is Absolute (Abundant) Light & Love, which is what you are at the Soul level. It is time to truly embody this within your Chakras and Energy Bodies.

It now becomes a Conscious Choice to Thrive, rather than just live in survival mode. It is a Conscious Choice to live in the vibrations of AND. It is a Conscious Choice to shift your paradigms and your consciousness to prosper and Thrive.

A Message from the Council of ALL

Greetings Dear Ones,

We invite you to give yourself permission to thrive within all aspects of your life. You do not have to choose to thrive in only one part, then sacrifice within another part. Thrive is an AND consciousness with an awareness and acceptance that you Truly can have it ALL.

It is allowing the etheric flow of your Divine birthrights to radiate throughout your energetic matrix. This is a merging of your etheric Diamond 'Light' Body within your physical existence and Physical Body on the planet.

In doing so, you allow your Soul to live within and through you, rather than it be a concept and separate from you. You are your Soul's Essence. In that, you will thrive, for the Soul knows not the need to survive, as your origination is Divine Love and the Infinite.

We love you so. Blessed Be.

Gem/Crystal for the Principle: Herkimer Diamond

The Herkimer Diamond is known as the King of the Crystals. It maintains a perfect state and never requires recharging.

This crystal brings forth purity, harmony, and Love. As you grow and evolve, the Diamond reminds you to manifest through the heart and Love. It is known as an attunement stone to instill trust, confidence, and abundance. It helps to activate and inspire your creativity, brilliance, and Genius Codes (and your Diamond Soul Codes of Destiny).

The Diamond vibrates to the Master #33: spiritual giving and that of the Christ-Grid consciousness spreading Light and Love.

The Universal Law of Cause & Effect

The Universal Law of Cause & Effect specifically states that every single action in the Universe produces a reaction, no matter what. Every single effect within our world, or upon our earth has a cause ... an original starting point.

All causes will have effects on anything and everything within the Universe, which then leads to further causes of other effects, and so the replication or chain reaction of events continue on Infinitely. To determine why something (or someone) has come into your life, you simply must search for the cause of the effect.

The elemental patterns of nature exist in balance. However, disturbances or shifts within these patterns (the cause) result in consequential alterations of the patterns of nature (the effect). For example, if the Physical Body is malnourished, it atrophies. The same is true on the spiritual plane. Nourishment results in strength — this is why meditation and prayer are key to you feeling centered, strong, and courageous even during uncertain times.

Every energy within the Universe is relative and interconnected; nothing is separate. Everything that exists within the Universe has always existed in one form or another. It is the microcosm of the Universe. The energy only shifts due to the intention and focus placed upon it. A movement, or an action cannot take place without its original thought (energy), or its preceding thought (energy). Any movement is the result of your thought (energy).

This is key and important to look for the source as to *why* you think, feel, believe, or act a certain way. The origination point begins with a chain reaction of events and creates further energetic derivatives, which extend out in all directions (within all aspects of your life). We are governed by the chain reactions of the interweaving of energy. There is a ripple effect out into the quantum field.

These continue to duplicate and replicate, which create your neuropathways that affect what is radiating throughout you and 'vibing' out into the world. As it ripples out into the Universe, it then returns to you (the source and Creator of the energy). Thus, YOU are the cause and effect within your own life.

This is why The Diamond Co-Creative System® and its Elevation Codes work, because they can help you to go to the *core origination* points of an issue (the cause), whether it be from your current or past life, lineage or genetic encoding, imprints, conditioning, or programming. It helps you to repattern the outdated energy to bring you current, thus shifting and reconfiguring your neuropathways.

There is an equal and matching reaction for every action, because of your thoughts, or the action from which it is derived. Therefore, it is specifically the intention that lies behind the action that must be addressed, if you are not receiving the results you desire. It is your intention behind the action that matters. We addressed this in the Prosperity Elevation Principle.

According to the Universal Law of Cause & Effect, nothing that happens is random or purely by chance. All output of energy (even if just a thought or feeling) or actions have consequences.

The consequences are neither good nor bad, but they may cause a positive or negative influence or effect on yourself or others, and your results. Hence, the saying, "You reap what you sow." Now, you understand the need for the paradigm shifts from survival to thrival, and to the AND consciousness.

The Universal Law of Pure Potentiality

The Universal Law of Pure Potentiality comes alive within you as you Consciously Choose to operate, create, and live within the 5th Dimension.

The source of all creation is Pure Consciousness whose Pure Potentiality seeks to express itself, bringing the potential from the etheric into a manifestation of physical form.

Create & Live
Your Diamond Life!

When you discover your True nature, which is your Diamond Divine-cell consciousness, you then have the power from within to manifest anything and everything in the Universe. As you come to know and align more deeply with your core Diamond Essence, you will have the ability to fulfill any goal or dream because you can tap into Eternal (Infinite) Possibilities and probabilities. You can Consciously Choose to create your Diamond Life!

What is a Diamond Life? A Diamond Life is the living and BE-ing the vibration and consciousness of LOVE ... Living Only Vibrant Energy. It is the fulfillment and manifestation of your visions and dreams in all facets of your life. It is the remembrance and return to the Diamond brilliance of your True Self, in both all that you are and do.

The Diamond within you is the brilliant facets of your Divine-cell consciousness. Your heart-centered Diamond power within you radiates forth your True essence, which is based on a foundation of Love. It allows your illusions and fears to fall away and claim the perfection that you already are.

Just as you are carbon-based in design within your biological/chemical human structure, so is a Diamond.

A Diamond is formed when carbon atoms bond with each other under high temperature and extreme pressure, thus transforming them into crystals.

Each carbon atom bonds to four other carbon atoms and continues to bond and lock into place with other groups of carbon atoms. Repeating this network, it eventually grows large enough to produce crystals that we can see. The end result ... the Diamond which is the hardest known substance on this planet.

Each Diamond is unique, with its multiple facets and colors, just as you are. From a meta (spiritual)-physical view, you are born as a unique 'Diamond in the rough.' Humans are more than 18% carbon and the air we breathe contains traces of carbon.

During this acceleration of time and space that humanity is going through, you are in an ascension process of upleveling into the 5th Dimension and beyond. You are transforming into more of a crystalline human structure, as your consciousness expands, and your vibrations rise into BE-ing more Love and Light.

You are merging and blending the spiritual and physical, becoming unified and One within, with others, and with the Universe. You are BE-coming your ALL ... Absolute (Abundant) Light and Love!

There are living examples today of those who radiate more from a foundation based on Love rather than fear and have more expanded Universal views and spiritual (not religious) ways of life, such as the Dalai Lama, Amah, and the Starseed Indigo, Crystal, Rainbow, and now the Diamond children. Their journey begins from within rather than from the outside of Self. They do not need validation, acceptance, or Love from the outside or others; it is all within first, which then vibrates forth.

Just like coal with its carbon atoms that form a Diamond via pressure and stress, we humans seem to create the same through crises, dramas, and chaos within our lives, all to lead us to embrace, create, and accept change. Some choose more drastic measures and circumstances: abuse, accidents, relationship losses, financial demise, incarcerations, disease or health crises, or even death of a loved one.

Some become regretful, unhappy, angry, resentful, spiteful, or blame others or their circumstances. Then one day, they combust, lash out, or project their pain upon someone, something, or with life in general. Up until then, they didn't listen to the whispers of their Souls or the Divine that change was needed. Thus, they get hit over the head with a 2X4 in whatever way the Universe can get their attention and many times in ways that will hurt the most, so one makes the decision to change.

When the dust settles, you have a choice to view this experience as an opportunity and a gift, to understand and learn from this life gem, and to heal the pain and the past. You have the choice to move forward in positive and powerful ways in which you can thrive and prosper.

As you continue your life's journey, you can Consciously Choose to explore the beauty of who you are and shine forth your Diamond Essence versus living out the conditioning, judgments, illusions, fears from the past, or what you think you are, or are not.

You can discover what (and even whom) has been 'running' your life. You can look at how you have shaped your life around illusional stories that you have created and what you have accepted within the illusions about your life, yourself, and others.

You can claim to allow and surrender into the Divine Truth. And you can own your destiny, your Divine Will, Divine Source's Love, and the abundance of the Universe, both inside and outside of you.

To do so, you must let go and shed the fears which have become your 'stories,' your illusions, your dramas, your masks, and your ego (Easing God Out). This is done by becoming authentic and intimate (Into Me I See) first with and within yourself, and then with others.

Being authentic means that you cultivate an awareness of what you are *really* thinking, feeling, saying, and doing. It is about being present with yourself in every moment and being willing to feel how life is showing up for you whether you like it or not, and whether you are comfortable with it or not. It is not about judging it, but rather accepting what is, is. It is about discernment.

Understand the carbon atom was already perfect, but it wanted to expand and create something new; it was claiming its Pure Potentiality. The carbon atom was a Diamond in the rough, but the rough was not about imperfection, it was just the next step in its potential and evolution.

It is the understanding that as with carbon atoms, you can intimately bond within yourself and with each other to create Love, beauty, and something even more brilliant. Or you can choose to separate, break down, and break apart from your True Essence and from each other.

You have within you what we call Diamond Soul Codes of Destiny packets awaiting to be opened. They reveal themselves and become apparent to you, when you are ready to take your next steps within your Soul's journey, purpose, and plan. They hold more of your Infinite Diamond Potential. Are you ready for one or more to open?

You can choose to discover the brilliance of your Diamond Essence and let your light shine forth! Living Only Vibrant Energy thrives through the acknowledgment and acceptance of your perfection in the moment and the eternal possibilities of your Pure Potentiality. You have at your calling the immeasurable Potential of ALL that was, is, and will be.

It is never too late and every step along the way has brought you closer to your fullest Potential, whether you realize it or not. You can Consciously Choose to do so now. You can Create & Live Your Diamond Life!

My Thrive Exploration

◊ What energy do I operate from ... survival or Thrival? What is its source and why?

◊ What aspects of my life can I shift into Thrival? Where do I Thrive and where do I not?

◊ Where do I play in the 'either/or' paradigm?

◊ How can I shift into the new 5th Dimension paradigm of AND?

◊ What thoughts, feelings, beliefs, and actions *Cause* the results that I no longer want?

◊   What are their *Effects* within various aspects of my life?

◊   What is my Pure Potentially that I want to claim?

◊   What would need to be the new *Causes* to create different *Effects*?

◊   Do I give myself permission to Thrive in ALL aspects of my life? If so, what paradigm shift do I need to make?

◊   Am I ready to claim my Diamond brilliance and life?

◊   What Diamond Soul Codes of Destiny packet am I ready to receive?

The Thrive Elevation Protocol

The *CCC ... Clear, Cleanse, and Calibrate* portion of the Thrive Protocol includes the Freedom, Forgiveness, Love, and Thrive Elevation Codes. These offer you the opportunity to release and transform your scarcity and lack patterns, and the need to just get by or to only survive. In doing so, you can then create and stand within the vibrations of thriving, regardless of what is occurring around you in your own life, as well as in the world.

You can Consciously Choose to dissolve your outdated consciousness and energetically complete what you desire within you and with others, and what no longer serves you when it comes to surviving in life, relationships, health, finances, career, and/or business.

The *EEE ... Energize, Elevate, and Evolve* portion of the Thrive Protocol includes the Love, Joy, Thrive, Freedom, and Trust Elevation Codes. By working and meditating with this Protocol, you will enter new spheres of co-creating with the Universe as it offers you Infinite Possibilities and SOUL-utions.

The energies of thrival, abundance, surplus, plenty, and even overflow become yours as you tap into the flow of the 5th Dimension and continue to strengthen and expand your Prosperity consciousness.

The Thrive Protocol Features
The Elevation Code of Thrive

Foundation   THRIVE   Creation

Thrive Elevation Code includes the Diamond Co-Creation Codes of
Foundation and Creation

The Foundation Code assists your Physical Body and your 1st Chakra
— Root. When your Root Chakra is out of alignment, your focus is on
surviving, and you are trying to create safety and security from outside
of you. You have a lack of trust that you will be provided for, and you go
into fear and lack/scarcity consciousness.

The Foundation Code assists you to shift from survival to thrival,
and from scarcity to prosperity. It helps you address deep seeded fears
and family belief systems that you may have taken on as your own especially about money and how you 'should' show up.

Plus remember if you don't address your fears then your Physical
Body will hold onto them and be affected by creating pain, stress, illness, chronic conditions, or dis-ease in order to get your attention. Thus,
working with the Foundation Code can help heal your Physical Body, as
it alerts you to the emotional release work that needs to be done.

The Creation Code works with your Astral Energy Body and your
2nd Chakra — Sacral. Your Astral Body is designed to protect your
Physical Body against physical threats. When it is out of alignment then

fear may be 'running' you all the time and it can hold more agitation and stress. When aligned, it will assist you to have more trust and faith.

You are always creating ... you are the Creator and Co-Creator in your life and what you manifest. So, what energy do you want to operate and create within? The Creation Code helps to tap into your heart-centered creativity guided by the Sacred Union of your Divine Masculine and Feminine within the 5th Dimension.

It helps you to transform the energetics of guilt, shame, plus issues with power, control, sex, money, and addictions within your 2nd Chakra. In doing so, you can create healthy, interdependent relationships with yourself, your Soul, others, and the Universe. Thus, Soul-aligned and Soul-inspired creations can be manifested, and you prosper and thrive beyond what you can imagine!

It is suggested to do the Thrive Protocol at least 2-3 times a week. Plus, as you activate the Elevation Code of Thrive, you'll discover your safety and security within as you claim thrival energetics and choose Prosperity consciousness. Activating the Elevation Code(s) on a daily basis helps you maintain these new ways of BE-ing!

The Thrive Protocol
(see next page)

The Thrive Protocol

The Elevation Codes	The Diamond Co-Creation Codes	Code's (S) Spiritual #	Code's (M) Mental #	Code's (P) Projection #	Purposes
CCC					**The Past & The Old**
Freedom	Expression & Power	8	9	8	Release, Clear, Cleanse, Transmute & Calibrate
Forgiveness	Compassion & Foundation	9	3	3	Release, Clear, Cleanse, Transmute & Calibrate
Love	Compassion & Connection	3	9	3	Release, Clear, Cleanse, Transmute & Calibrate
Thrive	Foundation & Creation	6	8	5	Release, Clear, Cleanse, Transmute & Calibrate
EEE					**5D – 5th Dimension**
Love	Compassion & Connection	3	9	3	Energize, Elevate & Evolve into the 5D
Joy	Compassion & Anchor	7	8	6	Energize, Elevate & Evolve into the 5D
Thrive	Foundation & Creation	6	8	5	Energize, Elevate & Evolve into the 5D
Freedom	Expression & Power	8	9	8	Energize, Elevate & Evolve into the 5D
Trust	Receive & Manifest	6	4	1	Energize, Elevate & Evolve into the 5D

The below is recommended verbiage. If you're guided differently, then go ahead and follow your guidance. The Codes 'know' exactly what you need and want.

CCC: (Name of Elevation Codes) Activate, Activate, Activate, Clear, Cleanse, and Calibrate, Calibrate, Calibrate, 44 Times Divine Source Speed at the 44th Power to Purify, Purify, Purify, my Chakras and Energy Bodies, so I can assimilate the energetics of Thrive within me and uplift into the vibrations of the 5th Dimension and align with my Highest Order and Infinite Diamond Potential.

Violet Flame … Transmute, Transmute, Transmute, 33 Times Divine Source Speed at the 33rd Power.

EEE: (Name of Elevation Codes) Energize, Energize, Energize, Elevate, Elevate, Elevate, Evolve, Evolve, Evolve 44 Times Divine Source Speed at the 44th Power and saturate every cell of my Being the energy of Thrive, so I Thrive in all aspects of my life and operate within the 5th Dimension and in my Highest Order and Infinite Diamond Potential.

CHAPTER THIRTEEN

The 5th Dimension Elevation Principle & Code of Soul

The Elevation Principle

SOUL … <u>S</u>ynchronized <u>O</u>neness within <u>U</u>nified <u>L</u>ove. You are more than your human body; you are Spirit incarnated, and it is your Soul's connection with its Divinity that Truly guides you.

SOUL ...
<u>S</u>ynchronized <u>O</u>neness within <u>U</u>nified <u>L</u>ove

It is in this lifetime that you have the opportunity to actually *embody* your Soul's Essence. It is part of your ascension journey. To 'ascend' means to fill your cells with Light, which transforms the denseness of your Physical Body and allows you to embody and BE your Soul's Essence. Thus, the result is the creation of your Diamond 'Light' Body within your Physical Body, which contributes to your ascension and continual evolution.

As you raise your frequency, your cells are filled with Diamond Light and Divine Love, and you move into the vibrations of the 5th Dimension and beyond. To ascend, you must release the negative, dense, low frequencies of outdated limiting beliefs, old emotional wounding, programming, conditioning, and imprints that you took on from the past or from others, throughout this lifetime and past lives.

You see, every thought, word, feeling, and action are vibrations that create your aura (your energy fields and matrix) and affect your Chakras and Energy Bodies. Ascension entails purifying and uplifting your thoughts, cleansing your emotional blocks and limitations, and choosing elevated and Loving ways of BE-ing and DO-ing until you radiate at a High frequency of Love and 5th Dimensional qualities. In this, you can then create and live continuously within the joy and freedom of your Soul's Essence and expression through you AND sustain a 5th Dimensional life!

Now, let's bring in the magic of synchronicity. Synchronicity operates in the 5th Dimension and beyond. Its 5th Dimension vibration provides the flow of energy that is aligned to Pure Potentiality and your Highest Order. Synchronicity can assist you in realizing a deeper connection to your Soul's purpose for this lifetime. It helps you tap into the vastness of your Soul and experience the Eternal Infinite spirit of who you are.

Many don't realize the role that synchronicity plays in their life. This is because they come from a sense of unworthiness, underserving, doubts, worry, and trepidations about who they are and what they are here to do. They live in vibrations of fear and separation. However, you have a Conscious Choice to release this way of living.

Let's break down the word Synchronicity: Sync and City.

You can sync up with your Beloved (YOU!), your Soul, and the Divine. As you do, you are synchronizing and harmonizing with the Heavens (the Eternal being you are, Love, and the Divine) and with the Earth (your Physical Body here on earth). Thus, you are creating "Heaven on Earth" within you, through you, and around you.

Sync is like the skies above, in which there are no bounds. It is to the Infinite heights that you can go. Sync is like the waves of the ocean, in which one wave flows into the next as it continues to the shoreline, the water then comes back out in the ocean to create more waves. The waves are like the vibration of synchronicity, which is endless, boundless, and in continuous flow.

Now, let's review City within synchronicity. Cities are built on a grid. Each city has its own grid structure, which is based upon what its origin is, where the city is, and how it is to serve its inhabitants.

You are your own city. You as a Spiritual Being within a human body are a city unto yourself. You have a golden grid in which you can stand upon:

- You have an origin — the Divinity of your Soul.
- You have a destination — your Dharma (Soul's purpose).
- You are here to be of service — the 'how' your unique gifts and talents are expressed through you.

The more you are aware of synchronicity, the more you will be in the flow within the 5th Dimension. The more you are open to receive, the more the Universe can bring to you.

As you become increasingly aware of the synchronicity in your life, you may be surprised at how easily something occurs. It may seem like magic to you, but it's really a natural occurrence that happens when you are connected to your Soul and operating from the 5th Dimension.

It's about recognizing the messages. It is about following the flow of energy within your Physical Body, from your Soul, and from your Spirit Guides and the Divine; they are always giving you clues. It is important to pay attention to and answer your Soul's calling and Divine purpose.

The magic of synchronicity is that there is REAL alignment. REAL ... Realized Energy Aligned with Love. There is a weave that occurs in the etheric which manifests into matter. There is the Universe orchestrating what's in your Highest Order and when you follow the energy, you are in flow; life, relationships, and business seem to be easier, gentler, and filled with joy and prosperity.

And it is you who is aligned with your Soul's energies to create the quantum field of Synchronized Oneness within Unified Love. It is your Soul's connection to your MORE and ALL ... Abundant (Absolute) Light and Love!

A Message from the Council of ALL

Greetings Dear Ones,

We honor you. We honor your willingness to be the unique expression of your Soul on earth at this time.

We invite you to honor yourself as well, to honor your uniqueness and all of who you Truly are. You are much more than what you see. You, as a multi-dimensional Spiritual Being, have the boundless Potential to manifest what you want and need.

We know some of you struggle, so we ask that you call upon us and relinquish your struggle, suffering, and pain. It no longer serves you, or humanity. At some point, we ask you to release the old way of learning and that of crisis as ways to bring about change in your life and others. This will no longer be necessary as you complete your past and your experiences within the 3rd Dimension.

We honor your healing and transformation, for in that you serve all of humanity by raising your vibrations and consciousness. Now is the time to move into expansion and the Higher Dimensions.

You are the Light and Love that humanity and your planet needs. You are your unique expression of your Dharma. We love and hold you in all that is possible ... individually and collectively. Thank you for choosing to be here and to be of service.

We love you so. Blessed Be.

Gem/Crystal for the Principle: Lemurian Seed Crystal

A Lemurian Seed crystal is a High frequency crystal that anchors in the Light. You can access vast knowledge and ancient wisdom that is held by the Lemurian Seed crystal by rubbing the ridges of the crystal.

It helps you to maintain your connection to Spirit and to your spiritual evolution. It has been used successfully in dream work.

It is a wonderful tool to use when clearing and activating the Chakras; it activates and connects you with all the higher Chakras (8th–12th) above the Crown Chakra. It is also used for healing and to create alignment with your spiritual path and your Soul's mission, purpose, and plan.

Vibrates to the #99 which is seen as the higher octave of the #9: wisdom, mystical, spiritual, completion, culmination, and humanitarian.

The Universal Law of Dharma

The Universal Law of Dharma means Purpose in Life. Each living thing has a purpose for its existence and a special experience to provide to this world. You have taken form to manifest within a human body to fulfill your Soul's purpose.

You, as a Soul, live in the field of Pure Potentiality (which was reviewed in the Thrive Elevation Principle & Code in Chapter Twelve). Pure Potentiality is Divinity in its Essence. The Divine takes human form to express itself and to fulfill a purpose.

Everyone has a purpose in life, a unique gift, or special talent to give to others. You have your own unique expression and only you can express it; no one else can do what you do. You have a distinct way of expressing what you came here to share.

There is no one like YOU. Revel in the joy of your uniqueness, rather than compare yourself with others. The other person is their own uniqueness and has their own Soul's journey. Theirs is not yours, and yours is not theirs. So, celebrate *all* of who you are!

You are here for a reason. You came here for a purpose … to be of service in your own unique way. When you blend your unique talents and expression in service to others, you can experience the ecstasy and exultation of your own Soul. When you help others for the greater good, your Soul will dance in joy.

You also have your own unique needs. When your needs are met through the creative expression of your talents, there is a spark. This spark fuels your prosperity and wealth as you fulfill the reasons as to why you are here and your purpose.

The most powerful questions you can ask yourself are:

- "What are my unique talents and gifts?"
- "How can I serve in the Highest Order?"

Focus on what you came here to experience and to give. It does not need to be grandiose. It can be as simple as BE-ing the Love you are and sharing it with all those you encounter. This may be in your family, with your friends, through your business, or simply by being out and about, and interacting with others in Loving and kind ways, showing that you care about them.

There are three components to the Law of Dharma:

I. Discover who you Truly are as a Spiritual Being having a human experience. Part of your Dharma is to realize and live as your Soul's Essence that is expressed through your personality. It is finding the God/Goddess within you … to operate from your Divine Masculine and Divine Feminine, which are 5th Dimensional and beyond frequencies.

II. Express your unique talents. Only YOU can do what you do! Only YOU can express it as you do! No one else can. It is as simple as this … BE YOU! When you do this, you will immerse yourself in what you're doing. You will lose your sense of time and space as you focus upon what you're here to do; in other words, you'll get lost in the joy of expressing your uniqueness in what you're creating and doing.

III. Be of service to others, humanity, and/or the earth. What did you come here to contribute? Ask yourself, "How can I help a person in each and every interaction I have with them?" Or ask, "How can I help the planet, what's mine to do?" When you come from this place rather than "What's in it for me?" (egoic mind and fear-based), then you are of True Service.

When you combine the three components with the experience of your own spirituality and the field of Pure Potentiality, you have access to boundless abundance. You will *always* and *in all ways* be taken care of as you live your Dharma.

You are an Infinite being and you can tap into the Infinite flow of abundance and prosperity at any time. Be open to 'how' it unfolds, which may be different from what you envisioned; the Universe will guide you into MORE of your Pure Potentiality. Be open to receive in the way the Universe wants to deliver. It has the bigger picture. Trust in the unknown as the Universe leads you to your ALL.

The most powerful thing you can do to change the world is to shift your own beliefs about your life and yourself, people, and humanity as a whole, into something more positive, and begin to act accordingly. You can set the Law of Dharma into motion by making commitments to the following:

- Love and nurture yourself, your Body, and all aspects of you–your Inner Masculine, Feminine, and Child by discovering the spiritual nature of who you Truly are. Develop a spiritual practice to discover and deepen within your spirituality … your connection with your Soul and the Divine.
- Open to embrace and allow for the flow of your Soul's Essence to embody within you. Carry the consciousness of the timeless Eternal being that you are in the midst of this time-bound lifetime experience.
- Set out to discover (or re-discover and expand) your unique talents. You may be aware of some, but are there more? Are there some gifts and talents that are ready for you to awaken, or to expand within you? In this process of discovery, allow for joy to flow within and through you. As you do, you will feel no sense of time.

Ask yourself, "How can I be of service to others, humanity, and/or the earth? With my unique talents and expression, how can I help serve the needs of others or the planet?" In doing so, you can get out of your own way by continually asking, "How I can help?" You will become a vibrational match to what you can provide with what others need by asking questions.

A way to go about this is to ask, "If I had all the time and money in the world, what would I do?" Is the answer the same as what you are currently doing? For many, it is, because they are living their Dharma … they exude their why and their passion. They wake up each day embracing what's next and what they can BE and DO during the day to be of service.

Express your unique talents and use them in the service of humanity, which will create abundance in your life as well as in the lives of others. Each day, ask yourself, "How can I serve? How can I help?" The answers to these questions will allow you to follow your Soul's guidance to help and serve fellow human beings in the vibrations of Love and service.

If for some reason you feel stuck, or feel like you've lost your passion or purpose, or you're bored with life or with what you're doing, here are two questions to help get your energy flowing again and for you to move forward:

- ◆ "What can I do today that will help me grow?"
- ◆ "What would Love do … how can I help another?"

Within you, there are Diamond Soul Codes of Destiny packets that are ready to be opened. As you step more into your Dharma, they will present themselves to you and ask to be opened. They hold more of your unique gifts and talents along with your Infinite Diamond Potential.

You have at your calling the immeasurable Potential of ALL that was, is, and will be. *It's never too late* and every step along the way has brought you closer to fulfilling your purpose and living your Dharma.

Remember, everyone has a purpose, including YOU. You can make a difference just by being YOU and exquisitely expressing your Soul signature and unique qualities!

My Soul Exploration

◊ How am I unique? List how you are different from others … not judging or comparing but reveling in that only you can be YOU!

◊ What are my unique gifts and talents?

◊   Do I value and honor my uniqueness? If so, how? If not, why?

◊   List the things I love to do while expressing my uniqueness.

◊   List the ways I connect with the spiritual aspect of me ... my Soul's Essence and Divinity.

◊   What is my daily spiritual practice to deepen the connection with myself and my uniqueness?

◊   How can I be of service with my unique talents, gifts, and expression?

◊   How can I help others each and every day?

◊   What synchronicities occur in my life that support me?

◊   How can I shift into the new 5th Dimension paradigm of being of service in all that I AM and do?

The Soul Elevation Protocol

Just a reminder, the Elevation Code Protocols are designed to make it easier and simpler to utilize the Elevation Codes of The Diamond Co-Creative System®. Two of the single Diamond Co-Creation Codes are combined within each of the Elevation Code. Each Elevation Code is ten-fold the potency and effectiveness of a single Code.

The name of the Protocol and the Elevation Codes reveal its purpose and how it can help you. As you get to know a Protocol and the Elevation Codes it uses, you can simply activate the Code or the Protocol. They will do their magic as you focus upon what your intentions are in using them and then identify what you need and want.

As in other Protocols the *CCC ... Clear, Cleanse, and Calibrate* portion of this Soul Protocol includes the Elevation Codes of Freedom, Forgiveness, and Love. The fourth Elevation Code within this *CCC* is Soul to help you clear any blockages in accessing and embodying your Soul's Essence.

Within the *EEE ... Energize, Elevate, and Evolve* portion of the Soul Protocol include the Love, Joy, Passion, Soul, and Trust Elevation Codes. We reviewed the other Elevation Codes other than Soul (see below) in prior chapters. Suffice to say, their names let you know the energetics they bring to you.

Allow yourself to tap into the Love and joy of your Soul's Essence. Tap into the passion of your Soul and its plan for you. And trust in the guidance of your Soul and in Divine Love.

Use this Protocol to assist you to clear any energetics, veils, or past lives that get in the way of you connecting with your Soul and your Soul's purpose and plan. Allow the Soul Elevation Code and Protocol to help you embody more of your Soul's Essence, so you can share and radiate it out your uniqueness into world!

The Soul Connection Protocol Features
The Elevation Code of Soul

Soul Elevation Code includes the Diamond Co-Creation Codes of
Grace (with the Silver Band) and Wisdom

The Grace Code with the Silver Band works with your 8th Chakra. Your 8th Chakra is the center that holds the pathway to your Life's Purpose. It gives you access to your Akashic records where the past, present, and future are held.

By accessing your past records, you can determine if there are incomplete energetic cycles due to any negative experiences, outcomes, and interpretations of them and you that you still hold. Then you can release, heal, and complete these cycles within the Akashic records and in this current lifetime. By energetically doing so, it will shift the energetics within you which has an effect on your present and future lifetimes. It will shift your way of BE-ing and DO-ing, thus your results.

The Silver Band brings forth the capabilities to magnetize and receive. It assists you to connect on a spiritual level and to utilize and listen to your intuition.

GRACE … Generating Radiant Actions Creating Eternity, assists you with allowing your Soul to guide you and for you to take Soul-aligned and Soul-inspired actions. Eternity energies are Universal Infinite energies which can create Soul-aligned Possibilities and SOUL-utions, even when you can't imagine the 'how' or what they would be. Allow Grace to be a guiding power to what's possible!

The Wisdom Code assists with your 9th Chakra. The 9th Chakra houses your Soul's blueprint which contains all your lessons learned with the knowledge and wisdom gained, your Soul's greater purpose, and Soul/Divine plan. This Code creates more Soul alignment … Soul-aligned thoughts, feelings, beliefs, perceptions, words, and actions. Thus, helping you to attain and sustain Higher Consciousness while you operate, create, and live within the 5th Dimension or beyond.

The Soul Elevation Protocol and Code can assist you to embody more of your Soul's Essence (energies) so that you are more Soul-aligned to create and manifest …

For Yourself: Soul — Synchronized Oneness within Unified Love
With Others: Soul — Serving Others within Unified Love

Remember to activate the Soul Elevation Code daily and it is helpful to use the Protocol 2-3 times a week as you focus on connecting with and embodying more of your Soul's Essence.

The Soul Connection Protocol
(Including Connection with Your Guides
& Your Dharma — Purpose)

(see next page)

The Soul Connection Protocol (Including Connection with Your Guides & Your Dharma – Purpose)

The Elevation Codes	The Diamond Co-Creation Codes	Code's (S) Spiritual #	Code's (M) Mental #	Code's (P) Projection #	Purposes
CCC					The Past & The Old
Freedom	Expression & Power	8	9	8	Release, Clear, Cleanse, Transmute & Calibrate
Forgiveness	Compassion & Foundation	9	3	3	Release, Clear, Cleanse, Transmute & Calibrate
Love	Compassion & Connection	3	9	3	Release, Clear, Cleanse, Transmute & Calibrate
Soul	Grace (Silver) & Wisdom	4	6	1	Release, Clear, Cleanse, Transmute & Calibrate
EEE					5D – 5th Dimension
Love	Compassion & Connection	3	9	3	Energize, Elevate & Evolve into the 5D
Joy	Compassion & Anchor	7	8	6	Energize, Elevate & Evolve into the 5D
Passion	Creation & Power	9	1	1	Energize, Elevate & Evolve into the 5D
Soul	Grace (Silver) & Wisdom	4	6	1	Energize, Elevate & Evolve into the 5D
Trust	Receive & Manifest	6	4	1	Energize, Elevate & Evolve into the 5D

This is recommended verbiage. If you're guided change, then do so. You can't do it wrong as the Codes 'know' exactly what you need and want.

CCC: (Name of Elevation Codes) Activate, Activate, Activate, Clear, Cleanse, and Calibrate, Calibrate, Calibrate, 44 Times Divine Source Speed at the 44th Power to Purify, Purify, Purify, my Chakras and Energy Bodies, so they can connect with and embody my Soul's Essence and Dharma within the 5th Dimension or Beyond and activate my Pure Potentiality.

Violet Flame ... Transmute, Transmute, Transmute, 33 Times Divine Source Speed at the 33rd Power.

EEE: (Name of Elevation Codes) Energize, Energize, Energize, Elevate, Elevate, Elevate, Evolve, Evolve, Evolve 44 Times Divine Source Speed at the 44th Power and saturate every cell of my Being to embody more of my Soul's Essence and expand my Soul connection within all aspects of my life and in the 5th Dimension or Beyond, and activate and fulfill my Highest Order and Infinite Diamond Potential.

CHAPTER FOURTEEN

The 5ᵗʰ Dimension Elevation Principle & Code of Trust

The Elevation Principle

TRUST ... <u>T</u>ruly <u>R</u>esonating and <u>U</u>niting with my <u>S</u>oul to <u>Th</u>rive. This is Truly a new level of understanding by embracing Trust in your life.

TRUST ...
<u>T</u>ruly <u>R</u>esonating and <u>U</u>niting with my <u>S</u>oul to <u>Th</u>rive

As you elevate more and more within the 5ᵗʰ Dimension, your doubts, worries, and concerns can be left behind. You can Trust that everything and everyone has entered your life for a reason. You can Trust that you too, are here for a reason.

As you 'own' your uniqueness, there is a wide range of new vistas that you can explore. And, as you continue to embody your Soul's Essence, you are aligning, resonating, and uniting with your True Essence, that of Pure Divine Love.

Imagine Trusting every choice, every decision, every unfoldment in your life that is leading you to fulfilling your Soul's purpose and plan. It can look messy at times. It can be daunting at times. It can even be confusing as you let go of what you've known before and enter into the unknown.

It can also be thrilling, ecstatic, and inspiring. You gain more and more freedom when you Truly Trust yourself and your Soul's journey. You gain the ability to see the MORE the Universe has for you as you Trust the process of your evolution and allow yourself to receive all of the gifts that await you.

When you Trust by 'owning' and knowing that there is a Divine reason for what and whom you've created and co-created in your life, you can be at peace within. When you Trust that all is in Divine Order and Timing, you surrender into your MORE. When you Trust that you are *always,* and *in all ways,* being taken care of by your Soul and the Universe, you can relax and live more fully into your ALL. You will resonate and unite with your Soul to thrive!

The Universal Laws of Unity, Change, and Magic will assist you in building the Trust within you. As you unify within and tap into the magic of the Universe, then you will Trust even more of what is occurring within and around you. You will Trust that "all is well," even if it does not seemingly feel that way for you at the moment. Over time, it will unfold, and you will recognize the gift in the challenges, and the blessings of the Divine.

You will Trust ALL of your Soul!

A Message *from* the Council Of ALL

Greetings Dear Ones,

We Trust you, so why not Trust yourself? Trust is actually a natural state of BE-ing as you are in the vibrations of Love and in the dimensions beyond your physical plane.

There is no doubt, worry, or concern fueled by fears when you claim Love. Fears are dissipated by Love ... Trust that this is Cosmic Law of the physics of the Universe. As you claim the Love that you Truly are, then Trust is inevitable.

We invite you to once again embrace your uniqueness. In this, Trust that you came to your planet earth with a design, a desire, and a plan to BE the change that you so seek within your world.

We Trust you to be that change. So, we beseech you to do the same ... Trust you and ALL that is!

We love you so. Blessed Be.

Gem/Crystal for the Principle: Lapis Lazuli

Lapis Lazuli are blue stones for the energy of Trust, as well as being the natural filter stones that block negative energy but allow positive energy to flow through. It was also a very popular stone for the ancient Egyptians who knew it as the 'stone of heaven.' Throughout the ages, Lapis Lazuli has been viewed as a stone of royalty decorating powerful kings, queens, dukes, and pharaohs who were secretly aware of the powerful effect Lapis Lazuli could have on the brain.

Lazurite, the main mineral component of Lapis Lazuli is a high vibrational stone. It opens your Third Eye to promote ascension, higher knowledge (and wisdom), and Truth-seeking. These attributes, combined with other mineral impurities (such as Pyrite, Calcite, and Sodalite), are all capable of reigniting different traits of who you are.

For example, *Pyrite* inclusions in Lazurite assist in both processing your thoughts and manifesting them into reality. *Calcite* variations will help awaken the mystical energies that lay dormant inside of you. Lastly, *Sodalite* will boost your mental insight to provide a True understanding of how your thoughts are connected to your Emotional Body.

You can find yourself radiating the Truth through your Emotional Body. It helps the communicative abilities between the mind, throat, and heart. Through meditation, you can understand your thoughts and sculpt your actions based on the knowledge that Lapis Lazuli has provided you.

Vibrates to the #3: joy, creativity, and connection to the trinity–Mother, Father, God/Father, Son, Holy Spirit/Heart Mind, Soul.

The Universal Law of Unity

The Universal Law of Unity ... we are all connected and all bearing the seed of Divinity. This is the way we start, and the way we develop as Eternal (Infinite) beings.

It is as you are in a physical form and operating within the 3rd Dimension that you feel a greater separation of your Higher Self (your Soul's expression) from your egoic-mind Self. The 3rd Dimension is where you experience the illusion that you are alone, and stand alone, which creates the thoughts, feelings, beliefs, and perceptions of separation.

Fears enter your Emotional Energy Body because of this illusion, which begins to close off your connection to Universal Source energy and to the Divine. Fear fuels distrust and does not allow what is Infinitely possible.

However, as you experience greater Soul growth, even in some small manner, it is profound and benefits all. All substances in this Universe flows to us and through us. We are ALL. There is Trust that "All is Well."

WELL ...
Wisdom (or Wealth) Energies aligned with Light and Love

The Universal Law of Unity recognizes that there is no separateness. It ignores the appearance and impression of separateness in the apparent divisions of polarities, gender, cause and effect, the part and the whole, the one and the many. This Universal Law realizes that each of these are the integrated parts of the total picture — the sum of the whole.

It identifies with the overall viewpoint, and it sees ...

- neither night nor day, but the night-day process.
- neither right or wrong, but the right-wrong process.
- neither the pleasure nor the pain, but the pleasure-pain process.
- neither the either/or, but the AND process.
- neither the one nor the all, but the At-One magical process of the ALL One Being, whose cells and Souls work together even in the seemingness of division.

This Unity Law acknowledges such division but stresses the Oneness of the parts. It sees loss and gain, or life and death as nothing but the spinning wheel of fortune that is based on the Universal Law of Change, which is itself a unified process known as the Universal Law of Magic.

The Universal Laws of Change & Movement

The Universal Law of Change states that, "The core of you, the Essence, the very Essence of Who You Are does not change." It continues on even as you assume different forms with different characteristics in different lifetimes.

Your Soul's Essence travels throughout the Omniverse, but the core of your being is constant, and in that too, your uniqueness prevails. Your Essence is in constant movement, even throughout what you think of as this lifetime. You are in constant movement.

There are times when you feel that you're at a still point in your creation and creative endeavors, but understand, in the still point, there is still the movement of creation and of re-creation. The Essence of Who You Are continues throughout time and space. That is the Universal Law of Change, and it elevates your logic to new levels, while knowing the *core* of you does not change.

With the Universal Law of Movement ... dreaming, inspiration, planning, implementation, action, fulfillment, repeated again and again, lifetime after lifetime, creation and re-creation (including letting go everything and everyone that does not serve you), your core remains constant. Who You Truly Are does not change no matter how many journeys you embark upon.

When you engage in working with change and continuity with the expression of your Divinity into form, it becomes a ripple effect. The Eternal flow of Love, peace, and gratitude creates the change with everything you are connected to, especially with the little things such as your smile, eye contact, and connection with another.

Take it to heart ... you are the change that this earth and humanity so desperately needs and wants at this time. As you accept and allow the simplicity of the Universal Law of Change, it creates harmonious flow in the Truth of change, constancy, and continuity, which energizes creations of Love, kindness, and peace. In that, "Heaven on Earth" is possible and is created for ALL!

The Universal Law of Magic

The Universal Law of Magic. Magic, when utilized with Love and honor, it creates the experience of Divine Union within yourself, with another, or with a group of others. In a state of Divine Union, the presence of 'God/Goddess/ALL That Is', fills each of those participating in the Union with Love. In doing so, each walks away from such an experience feeling Loved, joyful, blessed, connected, and fulfilled from within.

If magic is utilized without the energy of Love infused within it, then what is created is glitter or illusory without real substance or presence that can be dissolved in a moment. Therefore, it is important to be intentional and aligned with Love when you call upon the magic of the Universe to help you.

And remember the Universal Law of Faith that we Chapter Nine's 5th Dimension Principle of Love. FAITH … Freedom Aligned with Infinite Trust and Hope (or Happiness or Healing). Faith is founded upon the recognition that you know more than you have experienced, read, heard, or studied. You know more because you are more and a part of the ALL.

You have a direct link to Universal Wisdom. You are called to look within and to listen, so you can discern and Trust the guidance you receive from your own Soul and the Divine. As you do so, you develop more Trust in your own deepest intuition and wisdom. Trust is the final arbiter and Divine Source of your decisions.

To Trust is to 'know' what is in your Highest Order, Higher Purpose, and your Infinite Diamond Potential to evolve and live into your ALL … Abundant (Absolute) Light & Love.

My Trust Exploration

◊   What has Trust meant to me up until now?

◊   In looking at this new definition of Trust, how does Trust shift for me?

◊   How do I Trust me?

◊   How do I *not* Trust me?

◊   What evidence have I gathered to *not* Trust myself (or others)?

◊   In what ways do I Trust the Universe and in what ways *not*?

◊   What aspects of my life do I want to invoke more Trust?

◊   Do I Truly have faith and belief in myself and all that is unfolding within my life is in Divine Order and Timing?

◊ Where can I build more Faith in the changes that occur in my life?

◊ How can I embrace my evolution even more and Trust the process?

The Trust Elevation Protocol

The Trust Protocol includes the Trust Elevation Code within the *CCC ... Clear, Cleanse, and Calibrate* portion of the Protocol along with Freedom, Forgiveness, and Love. This will assist you to let go of any energy in which you distrust yourself, your Soul (and your Soul's plan and purpose), others, and the Universe. This includes releasing old emotional blocks and outdated thoughts and beliefs about yourself which have eroded trusting yourself.

With this Protocol, you can regain and build Trust of Self within and walk in the energy of Trust as you move about your day, live fully as YOU, and fulfill your Soul's destiny. It will also help you to let go of any resistance when a Soul contract is complete with someone or a situation and it's time to move on. You will Trust that all is in Divine Order and for the Highest Good for All.

In addition, with the Forgiveness Elevation Code, you can Truly forgive yourself for times in which you did not Trust your Soul or the Divine, or thought you made wrong decisions, mistakes, or failed. By forgiving you are able to complete old cycles of energetics and patterns that no longer serve you.

Included within the *EEE ... Energize, Elevate, and Evolve* portion of the Trust Protocol are the Love, Trust, Freedom, Harmony, and Balance Elevation Codes. You will learn more about the Freedom, Harmony, and Balance Elevation Codes in the next two chapters.

When you utilize the Freedom Elevation Code in both the *CCC* and *EEE*, you will become free of the past, conditioning, and programming deep within your cellular memory, so you can create the Freedom to Trust yourself and to be YOU. You Trust you can create the life YOU desire as you fulfill your Soul's plan. You Trust that ALL is Well.

The Trust Protocol Features
The Elevation Code of Trust

Trust Elevation Code includes the Diamond Co-Creation Codes of
Receive and Manifest

We reviewed the Trust Elevation Code in Chapter Nine's 5th Dimension Principle of Love but let's dive more into it.

Both the Receive and Manifest Codes work with your Third Eye — 6th Chakra … the Feminine and the Masculine aspects of your Third Eye, respectively. Feminine energy is the heart, gatherer, intuitive, feelings, emotions, and vision, while Masculine energy is the mind, thoughts, beliefs, protector, and provider, who manifests structure and form on this physical plane.

When the Feminine and Masculine can Trust one another, then magic can occur as they co-create together within Divine Union. You can build the energy of Trust within and around you.

The Receive Code with its Silver Band of receptivity also works with your Gravitational Energy Body. Again, this is the Energy Body that attracts and repels energies, opportunities, people, situations, and manifestations. When the Gravitational Body is in alignment with Love and your Soul-aligned plan, it will attract your fullest Potential, as well as repel anything or anyone who will distract you or take you off course.

When the Gravitational Body is out of alignment, it will attract the lessons that need to be learned, divulging your incongruent energies to what you desire, and manifests the 'what' and 'whom' in experiences and results that you don't really want. It goes out of alignment when another Energy Body is compromised by the past or old energetics such as within the Emotional or Mental Energy Bodies.

Address the issues and energetics that your Chakras and Energy Bodies are revealing to you that need to be healed and completed, then your Gravitational Body will come back into alignment with Love. Then you'll be back into flow and Trust to manifest your Infinite Potential.

The Manifest Code assists your Mental Energy Body. It helps you to shift your thoughts, beliefs, and perceptions into the 5th Dimension of your Soul-aligned thoughts, beliefs, and perceptions, which then also affect your emotions. Thus, this assists to elevate your consciousness to that of Trust, Unification, and Prosperity.

It has a Gold Band … the alchemy of manifestation, and the design band of Diamonds — your Diamond brilliance and the alignment with your Infinite Diamond Potential to help you easily manifest what you desire.

Utilize the Trust Protocol below 2-3 times a week or as guided. Plus, activate the Trust Elevation Code daily when you are integrating this Principle more and more.

This Code and Protocol helps you to become free and Trust yourself and the Universe beyond measure. You are so much more than your past, and Trust there's the MORE and ALL that's waiting for you to claim and BE!

The Trust Protocol
(see next page)

The Trust Protocol

The Elevation Codes	The Diamond Co-Creation Codes	Code's (S) Spiritual #	Code's (M) Mental #	Code's (P) Projection #	Purposes
CCC					The Past & The Old
Freedom	Expression & Power	8	9	8	Release, Clear, Cleanse, Transmute & Calibrate
Forgiveness	Compassion & Foundation	9	3	3	Release, Clear, Cleanse, Transmute & Calibrate
Love	Compassion & Connection	3	9	3	Release, Clear, Cleanse, Transmute & Calibrate
Trust	Receive & Manifest	6	4	1	Release, Clear, Cleanse, Transmute & Calibrate
EEE					5D – 5th Dimension
Love	Compassion & Connection	3	9	3	Energize, Elevate & Evolve into the 5D
Trust	Receive & Manifest	6	4	1	Energize, Elevate & Evolve into the 5D
Freedom	Expression & Power	8	9	8	Energize, Elevate & Evolve into the 5D
Harmony	Receive & Wisdom	3	8	11	Energize, Elevate & Evolve into the 5D
Balance	Gratitude (Gold) & Grounded	7	4	11	Energize, Elevate & Evolve into the 5D

This is recommended verbiage. If you're guided use different verbiage, then Trust your intuition and guidance. The Codes 'know' exactly what you need and want so you can't do it wrong.

CCC: (Name of Elevation Codes) Activate, Activate, Activate, Clear, Cleanse, and Calibrate, Calibrate, Calibrate, 44 Times Divine Source Speed at the 44th Power to Purify, Purify, Purify, my Chakras and Energy Bodies, so I can embody and align with the vibrations of Trust within myself, with my Soul, and with the Universe in the 5th Dimension.

Violet Flame … Transmute, Transmute, Transmute, 33 Times Divine Source Speed at the 33rd Power.

EEE: (Name of Elevation Codes) Energize, Energize, Energize, Elevate, Elevate, Elevate, Evolve, Evolve, Evolve 44 Times Divine Source Speed at the 44th Power and saturate every cell of my Being with the energy of Trust, so I Trust myself, my life, my Soul, and the Divine, and operate within the 5th Dimension and in my Highest Order and Infinite Diamond Potential.

The 5th Dimension Elevation Principle & Codes of Freedom

The Elevation Principle

Freedom is inherent within you. It is the vast spirit of who you Truly are, which can be expressed through you no matter who or what is in your life. It is your Divine birthright to be free.

FREEDOM ...
Flow into Remembrance to Embrace & Energize the Demonstration (or Discovery) of my Oneness & Mastery

You always have Freedom! It is always a Conscious Choice in what you think, feel, believe, say, and do.

Now, we're not saying that all freedoms are always possible; certain ones may not be due to others. Humans can lose their basic freedoms to those in power and control, or to those who have the need to be in power, such as within corporations or governments, wars, racism, gender discrimination, and so on.

In this 3rd Dimension paradigm and current world, there are many of these examples. You may feel your Freedom is being impinged upon by others (or even by society or governments).

But you have the Freedom to choose how you will *negatively react* or *positively respond in a neutral state of BE-ing.* You have the right to choose your own Freedom in any given situation, condition, or circumstance.

They cannot control what you think, feel, believe, say, and do. They cannot control who you are at your *core* … your authenticity and your Soul's Essence of Love.

This is the remembrance of who you Truly are … the Love, the gifts, the talents, and the expression of your Soul's Essence through your personality Self. And you can free your egoic mind and uplift in into your Divine Mind so you can explore the expansions and Freedoms that the Universe provides for you.

It is only YOU who takes your rights to Freedom away. You are the only one who may get caught up in your egoic mind, which, remember, has its own agenda for the need of perceived power and control over what is occurring within and around you. In doing so, it thinks it's keeping you safe and secure. Your egoic mind has a need to protect you from perceived threats.

Only YOU can control what is happening within your heart and mind. No one, and no thing, can control you despite what others may tell you. This is the Discovery and Demonstration of your Oneness and Mastery.

We have seen through ages of time how there are those who impose their wills upon others, who are attached to the perception that their way is the 'right' way, and who are afraid of the unknown and what they do not understand. They have taken away the physical freedoms of others.

However, they cannot take away who you Truly are. Only YOU can give this away. Only YOU can lose your inherent Freedom if you allow them to take your sense of Freedom away from you.

We have examples of those who stayed True to themselves even in the midst of invasions and war. The Dalai Lama is a good example who practiced the Mastery of compassion. As others took over the country in which he lived, he never wavered in his belief of Love and Compassion. He did not waver in the possibilities and beliefs of Oneness and Unity. He stood sovereign in his Freedom to BE himself and what he came here to demonstrate by setting his example of Love, compassion, acceptance, and grace.

When you think everything is someone else's fault, you will suffer a lot.
When you realize that everything springs from yourself,
you will learn both peace and joy.
— Dalai Lama

In the Elevation Principle of Love (Chapter Nine), we reviewed the Universal Law of Detachment. Detachment provides Freedom beyond measure as you allow yourself to be free from being attached to your outcomes. It also provides Freedom not to try to control or exert your power upon another person (or for that matter, even over another being such as a four-legged, winged, or finned one). It releases the struggle for power and control.

Here is a powerful excerpt from *Zen Thinking*:

Non-attachment is essentially a practice of presence and mindfulness. It is not allowing your sense of Well-Being to rely upon anything other than your own presence of awareness. It means to be in the world, but not of the world. A practice of non-attachment, however, doesn't affect how you appreciate, love, admire, and enjoy life. It simply means that your happiness is no longer defined by anything outside of you. In other words, you remain free!

Thus, it is your responsibility — *the ability to respond* — in claiming the Freedom you seek. It is your Conscious Choice to be FREE from the past, conditioning, and programming; use them as lessons and gifts in which you can grow, heal, and evolve. It is your Conscious Choice to be FREE in any given moment in time!

A Message from the Council of ALL

Greetings Dear Ones,

We invite you to remember who you Truly are ... that of Love and the Divine Spiritual nature of yourself. We invite you to lift the veils of forgetfulness and to allow your egoic mind to let go of what it knows and to surrender into the pools of your True nature, which is synchronized within the 5th Dimension and beyond.

Your Freedom is always available ... it is only you who chooses to give it up whether it be to your ego, to others, or to your societies, cultures, religions, or governments. Again, as a Spiritual Being creating a human experience, it is only you who allows others to take your Freedom.

Do you not understand those who struggle for their Freedom are here to learn that Freedom is within themselves, not outside of themselves?

And, yes, they are assisting to teach others that no one has the right to take another's Freedom away. It is complex, yet simple. Consciously Choose your Freedom rather than feel a bondage by another.

Consciously Choose to be the Mastery of yourself within Love and Oneness. Then you are always, and in all ways, to be Free.

We Love you so. Blessed Be.

Gem/Crystal for the Principle: Amazonite

Amazonite is called the Stone of Courage and Truth. It assists you to discover and access which helps empower you to search within and discover your own truths and integrity. It assists you to discover and access your inner Truth and personal power, allowing you to step into your authenticity and empowering you to live life to the fullest. It inspires hope, playfulness, and freedom with a care-free attitude.

Amazonite is also a stone of peace, harmony, and communication. It soothes the Chakras and aligns the Physical Body to the etheric. It is particularly rejuvenating to the Heart and Throat Chakras, enhancing Loving communication on all levels. It balances your Masculine and Feminine energies as well as many aspects of your personality Self.

Any environment that Amazonite is placed will calm the energy and fill the air with positive energies. It's called 'the peacemaker stone' due to its communicative abilities. You can enjoy more healthy and happier relationships by improving your communication skills and understanding others.

It encourages you to move beyond fear of judgment or confrontation with others and live in alignment with who you Truly are. It also allows you to let go of your limiting beliefs and emotional blocks, so you can tune into your intuition.

It provides the Freedom to express your thoughts and feelings. You can set strong and clear boundaries, both internally as Self-discipline, and externally as to what you're willing to experience. This assists you to be guided to make healthier decisions that lead to the joy and Freedom to be YOU!

Amazonite also empowers and strengthens any intention that may be infused within it; vocalize your desire while firmly holding a piece. It assists you in manifesting a path to your biggest dreams and desires as you let the Universe know what you want. Amazonite reminds you that you are in control of your own destiny with the Freedom to choose your decisions that will affect your outcome!

Vibrates to the #5: freedom, progressive, change, movement, and variety.

The Universal Laws of Free Will and Choices

The Universal Laws of Free Will and Choices give you the ability and Freedom to oversee yourself and the things you decide to do, or not to do. You may not be able to always control your circumstances, but you can control who you are BE-ing and what you are DO-ing amid any given situation.

Humanity has been given Free Will, the Divine Right to choose. Reclaim your power in making the choices that resonate for you. You actually control the *way* you will go down a path — how you think, feel, say, or do. This also gives you great responsibility as your choices have consequences. Your future is determined by the choices you make in the present moment.

You can choose how you're feeling, thinking, believing, speaking, and doing. You can choose *reaction* or *response*; you can choose to remain *neutral* despite what someone does, projects, or says. You can even be proactive and in charge of your own destiny, rather than being impacted or experience the aftermath of someone else's choices. Your life is the result of your Choices and your Free Will.

The Universal Law of Free Will has three parts:

I. Although many of the major events in your life are astrologically predestined, due to your birth chart, you always have the Free Will to mitigate the impact of an event, or to transcend it entirely. This will shift from how you live your life, prior to the time of the situation you've been destined to experience, so it can provide a different outcome. If you are positive, Loving, compassionate, and demonstrate by your actions that you have learned your past lessons, you can minimize any disharmonious or challenging experiences.

II. As you Master your conscious awareness and develop conscious detachment, you are far less affected by world events than you were in the past. As you develop your Mastery, you can enjoy all of the Love, warmth, and joy life has to offer. You can Consciously Choose to detach from negativity by allowing it to flow through you (or pass by you like a Tai chi movement) and not hold on to it, so it does not affect you in a negative way.

III. You always have Free Will to react or respond to any situation. If you respond with positive emotions — Love, compassion, and integrity, you've probably learned your karmic lessons and will not have to experience a similar situation in the future. However, if you have chosen not to learn, then your lesson will most likely continue and it will intensify until you choose to address the issue, heal it, and complete the energetic cycle.

The Universal Law of Choices lets you know that your decisions are made with your actions, not your words. It is Truly about 'walking your talk.' You can Consciously Choose to follow your intuition and inner wisdom from your Soul and the Divine, or you can resist it.

If you resist what your intuition is guiding you to do, in favor of instant gratification or the need to control and know, there can be consequences that result from your choices. Some of the choices may lead down an easy path, while others can take you down a path of challenges in which there are lessons to learn, but it allows you to grow spiritually and to evolve within your Mastery.

Eventually, you will be led back into alignment with all Universal Laws. You must recognize that each choice that you make, *either action or inaction*, and *consciously or unconsciously* will have consequences.

Your willingness to accept those consequences gives you the complete Freedom of Choice! You have the power to choose who you are, where you will be, and what you will do. No one, or no thing, can have power over you unless you give your power away or let them take it away.

Once you realize and accept this, then life changes from an obligation and a perceived reality, or that others or situations control you, to one of blessings which is full of Infinite Possibilities and opportunities. In that, miracles and Freedom occur!

You have choices and Freedom in *all* areas of your life such as …

- the feelings you decide to show or hold back.
- the quality of your thoughts to dwell upon.
- the beliefs you decide to follow and the perceptions that you have.

- the types of relationships you want to engage in.
- what foods you want to eat, what to wear, and how to express yourself.
- how you want to go through your day.
- the events you want to attend and not attend.
- the way you are with money and your finances.
- what your vocation is and what work you want to do.
- ways you want to contribute to others and the world.
- and so much more, the list goes on and on.

You even have the choice to step into your Soul's purpose and plan for this lifetime. You have the Free Will to accept or deny what you originally planned before you incarnated. Sometimes, the egoic mind, which may not be fully awakened yet, will block you from stepping into your power and Infinite Potential because of what it knows to be familiar and the fears it holds of the unknown.

It is YOU who must Consciously Choose different and decide that you will take the path of your Soul's calling and direction. It is always your choice; even the Divine or your Spirit Guides cannot mandate it otherwise.

Both the Universal Law of Free Will and Universal Law of Choices give you the opportunity to create Freedom within you and within all aspects of your life. You can Consciously Choose to BE free and BE your ALL!

My Freedom Exploration

◊   What does Freedom mean to me?

◊   How do I feel Free and how do I not?

◊   What do I need to Master in my life to feel Free?

◊   What am I choosing to BE in my life, relationships, and business?

◊   What am I choosing to DO in my life, relationships, and business?

◊   When there is a challenge, do I see the positive (the gift) or immediately go to the negative? If so, why?

◊ Am I typically in negative reaction, or in positive response?

◊ What situation or who triggers me? How can I shift to neutrality — what needs to be healed?

◊ What choices in the past do I deem as bad or wrong?

◊ What were the lessons and am I willing to forgive myself so I can create Freedom?

◊ What Freedom am I willing to claim as mine?

◊ What does my life look and feel like when I choose Freedom?

The Freedom Elevation Protocol

As a reminder, most protocols within the *CCC … Clear, Cleanse, and Calibrate* portion of the Protocol include the Elevation Codes of Freedom, Forgiveness, and Love. This will assist you to release the bondage to the past including other lifetimes, conditioning, programming, and lineage encodings. With the Forgiveness Elevation Code, you can Truly forgive and complete old cycles of energetics and patterns that no longer serve you and through this you can experience Freedom.

The *CCC* portion of the Freedom Protocol also includes the Balance Elevation Code which we will review further in the next chapter. However, it is important to understand how this Code can assist you in claiming your Freedom.

The Balance Elevation Code consists of Gratitude with the Gold Band and Grounded. These two assist in holding the space from the top to the bottom of your Chakra ladder. Gratitude works with the 12th Chakra (300 ft above your head) — Connection to Divine Source energies and to the Cosmos, while Grounded connects to your 10th Chakra (below your feet) — to stand upon a Divine Foundation which creates a firm footing in the vibration of Freedom.

This Protocol creates Freedom from the past and the Freedom to move forward in powerful and authentic ways. You can feel, think, and believe that you have a Choice within any given situation. It helps you to feel empowered in making decisions which are aligned with your Highest Order and Infinite Potential.

The *EEE … Energize, Elevate, and Evolve* portion of the Freedom Protocol includes the Freedom, Love, Joy, Thrive, and Balance Elevation Codes. As you create Freedom within you, you will experience MORE Love, joy, and balance which leads you into being able to thrive and prosper within your ALL … Abundant Light & Love.

Use this Protocol to BE Free and to become Freedom within every cell of your beingness. Give yourself the permission the Freedom to be YOU! Remember, it always your Conscious Choice to live and create within Freedom.

The Freedom Protocol Features
The Elevation Code of Freedom

Freedom Elevation Code includes the Diamond Co-Creation Codes of Expression and Power

The Expression Code works with your Karmic/Causal Energy Body, where all experiences in this lifetime and others are held, and it assists your 5th Chakra — Throat … your center of choice and voice. You can Truly let go of the past if you're willing to address any past experience or past life bleed throughs that you deemed negative, so you're no longer being affected by them. This allows you to be free of the past; you can then make choices in the present moment rather than bound to the past.

This Code can help you open your voice to allow for your Soul's Essence to flow through your personality Self. You can use your voice in authentic ways, which are aligned with your Divine Truth and the expression of your True Self, without couching or suppressing the power and Diamond brilliance of yourself.

The Power Code assists the Spiral Energy Body, where your family imprints and Genetic and Lineage Encodings are held. By utilizing this Code, you can release imprints and encodings that are not yours and can get in the way of your Soul's purpose and plan. You are then Free to be YOU and be in your own energies, rather than be impacted by your ancestors and others.

The Code also works with your 3rd Chakra — Solar Plexus, which is your center of power, Self-esteem, and will. This helps prevent you from giving your power away to others, money, a job, or situations. If you are afraid of power and fear your own power, then the Power Code can help reveal the underlying causes and core origination points of the fear(s).

As you heal and realign to the energy of your heart-centered power, then you can tap into and claim the innate power and wisdom that you hold within your Soul and cellular memory. Thus, you can feel and know the power of who you Truly are and the power of your Conscious Choices!

Activate the Freedom Elevation Code on a daily basis and if you feel stifled or constrained energetically during the day, activate it again to remind yourself you are Free!

Below is the Freedom Protocol and utilize it 2-3 times a week as you integrate this Principle and anytime you want to create more Freedom within you and your life.

The Freedom Protocol
(see next page)

The Freedom Protocol

The Elevation Codes	The Diamond Co-Creation Codes	Code's (S) Spiritual #	Code's (M) Mental #	Code's (P) Projection #	Purposes
CCC					**The Past & The Old**
Freedom	Expression & Power	8	9	8	Release, Clear, Cleanse, Transmute & Calibrate
Forgiveness	Compassion & Foundation	9	3	3	Release, Clear, Cleanse, Transmute & Calibrate
Love	Compassion & Connection	3	9	3	Release, Clear, Cleanse, Transmute & Calibrate
Balance	Gratitude (Gold) & Grounded	7	4	11	Release, Clear, Cleanse, Transmute & Calibrate
EEE					**5D – 5th Dimension**
Freedom	Expression & Power	8	9	8	Energize, Elevate & Evolve into the 5D
Love	Compassion & Connection	3	9	3	Energize, Elevate & Evolve into the 5D
Joy	Compassion & Anchor	7	8	6	Energize, Elevate & Evolve into the 5D
Thrive	Foundation & Creation	6	8	5	Energize, Elevate & Evolve into the 5D
Balance	Gratitude (Gold) & Grounded	7	4	11	Energize, Elevate & Evolve into the 5D

This is recommended verbiage. If your Guides or Soul change it for you, then follow the guidance. The Codes 'know' exactly what you need and want even if you don't.

CCC: (Name of Elevation Codes) Activate, Activate, Activate, Clear, Cleanse, and Calibrate, Calibrate, Calibrate, 44 Times Divine Source Speed at the 44th Power to Purify, Purify, Purify my Chakras and Energy Bodies, so I feel the Freedom to BE me and express who I Truly am through my Soul's Essence in all of life and in the 5th Dimension.

Violet Flame ... Transmute, Transmute, Transmute, 33 Times Divine Source Speed at the 33rd Power.

EEE: (Name of Elevation Codes) Energize, Energize, Energize, Elevate, Elevate, Elevate, Evolve, Evolve, Evolve 44 Times Divine Source Speed at the 44th Power and saturate every cell of my Being the energy of Freedom, so I feel Free to BE me and express my authentic Self, while I operate within the 5th Dimension and beyond and in my Highest Order and Infinite Diamond Potential.

The 5th Dimension Elevation Principle & Codes of Harmony & Balance

The Elevation Principle

Harmony and balance are found within the Infinite energies of the Universe. As you are an Eternal (Infinite) multi-dimensional Spiritual Being, you have the ability to always be in balance within the harmony of the Infinite, at any time.

Divine harmony and balance are found within the Infinity symbol. The flow of energy pulsates from the center point back and forth, or in and out of the center. It holds the All-knowing cosmic rhythm of the Universe and the brilliance of the ALL Absolute (Abundant) Light and Love.

The Infinity symbol is a bridge between your physical presence on the earth and your Soul's Essence, the Divinity of you. When you are connected in this way, you will think, feel, and see people, events, and situations within a different 'light.' You have a 'knowing' that there's much more occurring than you can imagine due to the limitations and constructs of your egoic mind. The more you utilize the Infinity symbol, the more you can tap into the Infinite Possibilities and SOUL-utions that await you.

It is why we utilize the Infinite Divine Breath meditation (Chapter Seven) to connect you with the spiritual and the physical, and to connect your heart and mind to the Infinite quantum field of the Universe. This also allows the flow of harmony and balance to occur within you, as well as within your life and the world.

Balance can only occur when you feel harmony within. To obtain a state of harmony, it is important to release any energy (even anyone or anything) which is incongruent with your vibrations. In doing so, you become congruent with who you Truly are, and there is a concordance that is consistent with the whole of you.

You feel a sense of balance created within you, which is then reflected outside of you. This often feels like a sense of peace regardless of what is occurring around you or in the world.

Only you can create this harmony and balance. It is always, and in all ways, your Conscious Choice to decide what works for you and what does not, and what serves you and what does not. If you find yourself caught up in the fray of what's occurring in the world, or you feel deeply affected by others and their choices, you can choose to focus on your own inner peace and harmony.

If you allow yourself to be triggered by what others say or do, or by situations, then it's up to you to make a different choice and go within to address what's occurring for you. You can choose peace, harmony, and balance within you and in any aspect of your life, relationships, health and well-being, finances, career or business.

It is why we have given you the Universal 'L' from The Diamond Co-Creative System® to assist you to invoke the Infinite …

The Universal 'L' contains three Infinity symbols within its design. Its purpose is to provide the energies of Universal Love and Co-Creation. It goes beyond the scope of any current circumstance and transcends the energies to provide the Highest Order and greatest potential for All.

This is a tool that is typically underutilized. We ask you to trace the Universal 'L' within yourself to vibrate Universal Love and Co-Creation out into the world. Do this every day for yourself, then share it with others.

Envision sending out the 'L' out to your sphere of influence: friends, family, clients, to those you do not even know, and even to people currently in power in governments, corporations, and countries. Send the 'L' to wherever there is discord, upheaval, or natural disasters, and to the lands, to the waters, to the animals, and even out into the cosmos to create Love and the Highest Order of All.

Why? The Universal 'L' can assist you and others to transcend any energy, circumstance, or situation. And you are a Master Co-Creator and Creator! We ask you to co-create Love, no matter what, or whom. In this way, you help to create balance and harmony within you as well as in the world. You can be the change by assisting the Unification process and uplifting humanity into Love and Oneness.

Check page 204 for the Resource Hub to download a free Universal 'L' e-Book.

A Message from the Council of ALL

Greetings Dear Ones,

We beseech you to choose Love in any given situation. If you do so, you will discover the harmony and balance that Love provides. Remember, this is no longer a lifetime in which you must suffer or struggle. You came to your planet earth to experience the presence of Love and joy, even amidst chaos and discord.

We understand that this might be difficult for you to comprehend but trust us in knowing it can always be so. By invoking the Infinite, you will always be guided to what is in the Highest Good for All.

By summoning the Infinite, you are calling forth Love and the Divine to intercede. By calling forth the Infinite, you can find harmony, balance, and peace within, regardless of whom is in your life or what occurs around you.

As always, and in all ways, it is your responsibility and your Conscious Choice to choose what you Truly desire. As they say in your world, "Do you want to be right or happy?" It's a choice. And we ask you to choose from the Love that you Truly are, and from the wisdom of your Soul which are both Infinite. It is already within you.

We love you so. Blessed Be.

Gem/Crystal for the Principle: Topaz & Clear Quartz

Topaz is the stone of calm and balance. It promotes kindness, compassion, and empathy. Topaz can help enhance awareness, relieve tension, and encourage feelings of joy. Traditionally, it was favored by scholars and artists because it was believed to aid in Higher thinking.

Clear Quartz promotes Love and joy by removing negative energy and infusing positive Light. It is one of the best crystals for joy because it brings High vibrational healing Light into your Body and raises your vibration, so you can attain the Love and joy you desire.

It is known as the Master Healer and attunes the Heart and Third Eye Chakras to Love. It helps to purify your Energy Bodies — Physical, Emotional, Mental, and Spiritual, and all Chakras to activate and create alignment and flow. It was used in Atlantis and Lemuria for healing, rejuvenation, and expansion.

It connects you with the Higher realms, clears your mind, and helps you achieve your intentions. Clear Quartz hums with High vibrations, which sweeps away all traces of negative energy and magnifies even the smallest intention. If you feel backed into a corner, or in lower frequencies, utilize your Clear Quartz to infuse you with a new perspective and claim a new lease of life. Allow it to guide you to a more harmonious alignment with Light and Love.

Clear Quartz amplifies the energy field in the location in which it resides and provides magnification of energy fields. It is a transmitter and receiver of information and energy from the spiritual realms. It assists in the creation of power and provides you with clarity and connection between the physical plane and total Universal Consciousness. It can be used to harmonize and align human energies with the energies of the Universe.

It vibrates to the #4: builder, organizer, stabilizer, unifier, and being of service.

The Universal Law of Balance

Let's begin with the Universal Law of Balance or Equipoise (fair exchange). This is an elaboration and continuation of the Universal Law of Equalities. The Law of Equalities, otherwise known as the Principle of Essential Divinity, is "As above, so below; as below, so above."

The major linking agent in the Universe is the energy of Infinite Love-Wisdom, and its purpose is to lead the egoic mind back toward the sense of Oneness (enlightenment). The thoughts and images you hold in your conscious and subconscious mind will manifest their mirror likenesses in your external circumstances. Your outer world is a mirror of your inner world due to the vibrations radiating within you, thus vibrating out from you.

The Universal Law of Balance supersedes all man's laws, creating stability for all 3rd Dimension manifestations. When you allow your thoughts to be in balance, you are invoking Divine Wisdom.

In doing so, you can allow all viewpoints; you may not agree but you understand each person has a right to what they believe. You are in observance and you don't feel that you must defend your own; you just take a stand in what's True for you.

You allow no one to tell you what your journey must reflect, or what your reality is. And the same is true for others; their journey is theirs, not yours. In this, you do not give your power away to others or circumstances. But you do give your Love without conditions and without expectations.

Any messages communicated in Infinite Love validate equality. Any communication sourced through low Self-esteem or the egoic mind is nonproductive; it's just a 'puffed-up' sense of Self, "I know best," "I'm right, you're wrong," my way or the highway, or spiritual righteousness. As such, they all deny equality, harmony, and balance.

Another manifestation of imbalance is addiction. You can be addicted to many things, such as alcohol, drugs, food, shopping, sex, work, but also to drama, chaos, crisis, confusion, uncertainty, pain, suffering, struggle, need for control, or the misuse of power. These often come from past conditioning and programming such as co-dependency which need to be healed.

When you are afraid, or fear is 'running' you, it can fuel any one of these addictions. Fears and addictions contribute to internal and external disharmony, resulting in an imbalance within oneself, one's life, and interactions with others, which is subsequently projected out into the world and becomes your skewed reality.

The Universal Law of Balance also states, "for every action, there is a reaction." The energy of the Universe is continuously flowing from action to reaction, and in search of harmony to achieve balance. This brings us to the Universal Law of Harmony.

The Universal Law of Harmony

The Universal Law of Harmony ... everything must be in harmony with other aspects of the Universe. This includes within yourself and with others.

Thoughts about others create cords of energy that extend from the source of thought to the individual that one is thinking about. If the thought is one founded within the vibration of Love, then it creates a positive vibration and a positive connection.

If it is out of alignment with Love such as projecting your fears, imposing your will upon another, judgment, criticism, or upsetting, it creates a negative cord. This disturbs the inner peace and harmony of the one who initiates the energy ... the thoughts, the feelings, the beliefs, the words, and the actions. And it may impact others depending on their level of emotional and spiritual maturity.

In maintaining a state of harmony and peace, all such cords sent to another must be returned to their source of origin (the person who sent them). If you are the one who casts out the negative thoughtforms and projections, you are responsible for your own disharmony and imbalance as well as that within the relationship. This creates cords from one to another.

If it is you, then you must do the work and clean it up energetically within you and karmically with yourself and the other. If you are receiving these energies from another, then you have the choice to take it on and react to it, or to remain neutral and balanced within your own harmony.

To create internal harmony, it is important to learn how to set boundaries, so you do not allow others to trespass upon your energy fields and your own thoughtforms. In doing so, any judgmental thoughts cast to you will cease to be 'a part of your reality.' You will no longer take it personally, and you will let them pass by you. It takes emotional and spiritual maturity to make a different choice and not give away your power or be a victim to others or circumstances.

It is the Conscious Choice that your harmony and balance is *more* important to you than someone else's opinion, or the need for their Love, acceptance, and approval. These are old codependent and 3rd Dimensional needs and habits. Cords can be created through these energetics and the wounds and fears you may hold.

Cords are also the result of attachment; someone is attached to a certain outcome. Once you have identified a negative cord and its source, severing the cords and returning them to their source of origin without any judgments is key. When you do so, you can begin to attain a True state of non-attachment.

In a state of non-attachment, you begin to "live in the world, but not of the world." You can maintain an inner state of peace, harmony, and tranquility. You are also able to maintain a state of harmlessness in all that you are and do; you are mindful of your own thoughts, perceptions, feelings, and projections.

Practicing and living in peace, harmony, and balance is a discipline and a choice in Higher consciousness and actions. The choice is always yours: Love or fear, High or low vibrations, and separation or Unity within yourself and with others. Consciously Choose to live in the ALL ... Absolute (Abundant) Light & Love!

My Harmony & Balance Exploration

◊ Where in my life am I in Harmony, and where am I not?

◊ What (or whom) is the cause and effect of my Harmony or disharmony?

◊ Where in my life am I in Balance, and where am I not?

◊ What (or whom) is the cause and effect of my Balance or imbalance?

◊ What (or whom) am I judgmental about and why?

◊ Do I project my fears upon others? If so, what are these fears and what are the projections?

◊ When, or how, do I try to impose my will or opinions upon others, or out in the world?

◊ In doing any of the above — judgment, projections, imposition — how does this take me out of Balance?

◊ To what (or whom) am I attached?

◊ What can I do to create detachment in my life, relationships, or business?

◊   What boundaries do I need to put in place …
    Personally?
    Professionally?

The Harmony & Balance Elevation Protocol

The Harmony & Balance Protocol includes the Elevation Codes of Freedom, Forgiveness, Love, and Harmony within the *CCC … Clear, Cleanse, and Calibrate* portion of the Protocol. This will assist you to release any disharmony that you hold within yourself or with another and create sustainable transformation.

Judgments, attachments, and upsets can cause you to be out of harmony, which creates you feeling 'off' and out of balance. When this happens, you have dropped into lower vibrational thoughts, feelings, and beliefs. Your mission, if you so choose it, is to move from disharmony back to Love. Love transcends All.

Remember, with the Forgiveness Elevation Code, you can Truly forgive yourself, others, a situation, your Guides, and the Divine which brings you back into harmony and balance. Let go of being right, being in control, or imposing your will upon another. Forgive yourself when you do so. And forgive others who try to do the same with you. By doing so, this will complete old energetics and karmic cycles that no longer serve you.

Plus, the Harmony & Balance Protocol works magnificently with the Forgiveness & Peace Protocol, especially if you have difficulty with letting go and getting out of fear, judgments, or projections. And the Freedom Protocol can assist you to create non-attachment so you can easily choose harmony and balance.

The *EEE … Energize, Elevate, and Evolve* portion of the Harmony & Balance Protocol includes the Love, Joy, Trust, Harmony, and Balance Elevation Codes. As you build trust within you, it is easier and quicker to choose harmony and balance. We have already reviewed Love, Joy, and Trust in other chapters, so we will dive into the Harmony and Balance Elevation Codes.

The Harmony & Balance Protocol can lead you to the peace that you may be seeking. When you are at peace within, then you are at peace with others and the world. You can be your ALL … Absolute Light & Love!

The Harmony & Balance Protocol Features
The Elevation Codes of Harmony & Balance

HARMONY

Receive

Wisdom

Harmony Elevation Code includes the Diamond Co-Creation Codes of Receive and Wisdom

The Wisdom Code works with your 9th Chakra. Your 9th Chakra holds your Soul's blueprint with your total skills and abilities learned in all lifetimes, plus your upgraded Cellular Memory blueprint. It provides you with access to your greater Soul's plan and purpose, and your fullest Potential.

The Wisdom Code assists you to access what is in your 9th Chakra and gives you the opportunity to allow your Soul's wisdom to come forth. It is also a bridge to connect you with the Divine wisdom you have already embodied, as well as the new information that the Divine and your Soul wants to share with you.

When the Wisdom Code works in tandem with the Receive Code which assists your 6th Chakra — Third Eye, you can access your innate wisdom from your Soul and the Divine. You can receive this wisdom through your intuition and opening to the visions held in your 6th Chakra. With access to your wisdom, you can then practice discernment versus judgment. You can trust what's True for you and in your Divine Order.

The Receive Code also helps you to connect more easily with the intuitive part of you and your Clair-gifts. As you listen to and trust your intuition more, you will enjoy more awareness and mental clarity. In addition, the Code expands your capacity to tap into the Universal Mind and Higher Consciousness.

The Code also works with your Gravitational Energy Body. When the Gravitational Body is in alignment with Love and your Highest Order, it is easier to attract and manifest what you desire. You find yourself in more 5th Dimensional energies in which flow and synchronicity occurs. When in alignment, it will also repel energies, situations, or people you don't need and don't serve you in your life.

When the Gravitational Body is compromised by other Energy Bodies and Chakras, it will go out of alignment. When this is so, you attract the lessons you need and create wisdom from these experiences. Rather than be upset by the lesson or challenge, embrace it so you can learn, grow, and evolve.

Balance Elevation Code includes the Diamond Co-Creation Codes of Gratitude (with the Gold Band) and Grounded

The Gratitude and Grounded Codes are assisting you to hold the space from top to bottom — 12th Chakra 300 feet above your head and the 10th Chakra — below your feet respectively. Gratitude helps with the connection to Divine Source, to the Cosmos and beyond, and to your advanced spiritual skills beyond what you currently know. It holds Unity Consciousness and helps you with your ascension within the Physical Body.

With the Gold Band, it provides an alchemical process of manifestation. And, with the energy of Gratitude you are now in one of the Highest vibrations within the Universe. Gold also provides the energetics of the Master Healer which makes it easier to heal and transform.

The Grounded Code assists you to create a Divine foundation for you to stand upon within the 10th Chakra. With Grounded, it helps the 10th Chakra unlock your unique skills contained in the 9th Chakra and creates a Legacy consciousness with Divine Christ-like/Buddha energetics.

It also assists with Unification and embodiment of your Divine Masculine and Feminine, and your Soul's energetics within. It helps the flow of Divine creativity through the synchronicity of life, while grounding your Divinity within your Physical Body and physical manifestations.

You will experience how this Elevation Code work hand in hand, beautifully and powerfully, with the Harmony Elevation Code. Create the peace you desire with these Elevation Codes!

On the next page is the Harmony & Balance Protocol to use 2-3 times a week as you work with this Principle. Plus, activating the Harmony and Balance Elevation Codes daily as you work with this Protocol helps you to harmonize your inner and outer worlds and to keep balanced in your life.

The Harmony & Balance Protocol
(see next page)

The Harmony & Balance Protocol

The Elevation Codes	The Diamond Co-Creation Codes	Code's (S) Spiritual #	Code's (M) Mental #	Code's (P) Projection #	Purposes
CCC					The Past & The Old
Freedom	Expression & Power	8	9	8	Release, Clear, Cleanse, Transmute & Calibrate
Forgiveness	Compassion & Foundation	9	3	3	Release, Clear, Cleanse, Transmute & Calibrate
Love	Compassion & Connection	3	9	3	Release, Clear, Cleanse, Transmute & Calibrate
Harmony	Receive & Wisdom	3	8	11	Release, Clear, Cleanse, Transmute & Calibrate
EEE					5D – 5th Dimension
Love	Compassion & Connection	3	9	3	Energize, Elevate & Evolve into the 5D
Joy	Compassion & Anchor	7	8	6	Energize, Elevate & Evolve into the 5D
Trust	Receive & Manifest	6	4	1	Energize, Elevate & Evolve into the 5D
Harmony	Receive & Wisdom	3	8	11	Energize, Elevate & Evolve into the 5D
Balance	Gratitude (Gold) & Grounded	7	4	11	Energize, Elevate & Evolve into the 5D

This is recommended verbiage only; if you're guided to use something different then honor the guidance. The Codes 'know' exactly what you need and want.

CCC: (Name of Elevation Codes) Activate, Activate, Activate, Clear, Cleanse, and Calibrate, Calibrate, Calibrate, 44 Times Divine Source Speed at the 44th Power to Purify, Purify, Purify, my Chakras and Energy Bodies of any disharmonies or imbalances, so I may feel harmony and balance within me and with my Soul in the 5th Dimension.

Violet Flame … Transmute, Transmute, Transmute, 33 Times Divine Source Speed at the 33rd Power.

EEE: (Name of Elevation Codes) Energize, Energize, Energize, Elevate, Elevate, Elevate, Evolve, Evolve, Evolve 44 Times Divine Source Speed at the 44th Power & saturate every cell of my Being with Divine harmony and balance as I create and live my ALL within the 5th Dimension fulfilling my Highest Order and Infinite Diamond Potential.

CHAPTER SEVENTEEN

The 5th Dimension Elevation Principle & Code of Abundant

The Elevation Principle

Abundant is a state of BE-ing. To attract abundance in your life, it is imperative that you *feel* abundant within every cell of your beingness and within your consciousness.

This not only elevates into Prosperity consciousness, but it will help you obtain an *Abundant* Prosperity consciousness. This adds the attribute of the Infinite and the ability to manifest in the physical world while you operate, create, and live within the 5th Dimension and beyond.

Just as there is no energetic space for Love when fear resides in your thoughts, feelings, and beliefs the same is true with lack and abundance. If you continually think about what you *don't have*, or believe there's not enough, that's exactly what you will create and manifest. If you only focus upon lack or scarcity, then the abundance the Universe has to offer you cannot come to you. If you only play in survival mode, you cannot thrive.

We would ask you to 'reframe' your scarcity, lack, or not enough thinking to that of being grateful for what you *do* have. To create more abundance, build upon the gratitude of what's here in the moment for you, even if it's only one small thing in your life or a small amount in your bank account. In that, the Universe can answer your call, "Thank you for this and I want MORE. I am open to receiving my ALL!"

It is always, and in all ways, your choice as to where you focus your attention. This reframe shifts your lower vibrational lack consciousness to that of 5th Dimension Abundant Prosperity consciousness.

What is the vibrational match to that which you desire? Remember, lack attracts lack, or abundance attracts abundance. The Universe will always answer your call; it may look different than what you think, but aren't you always provided for and have what you Truly need?

Know that the Universe always sees what you need and want. Trust that the Universe will always provide for you, but maybe in ways you have not even considered or imagined.

In the past, you may have been driven by "there's never enough," so you strive to need and want to have more but it's motivated through fear. You may also have a need to prove you are worthy and deserving of Abundant Prosperity. This is old 3rd Dimension paradigm conditioning and programming.

The MORE and ALL are actually your Divine birthrights, so there is nothing 'wrong' with asking for more. And the MORE is really a 4th Dimensional energy that still has limitations within it but it provides the path to Moving Onward Respecting Eternity (the Infinite). There can still be an energy of not enough, or not quite enough in the MORE. But at least you are moving in the right direction and asking for what you want and need.

It is asking for the ALL that you step into the 5th Dimension of Abundant Prosperity and of course, Abundant Light and Love.

We would ask you to be driven by ...

+ What is my Soul-aligned creation and manifestation?
+ What does my Soul want and hold for me?
+ What does my Soul know that's within my Divine Plan for this lifetime?
+ What does my Soul want to share with me and what does it want to experience?
+ What is the ALL that the Universe wants to give to me?

Your prayers and your intentions are the ways you can plug into the Divine's Infinite Possibilities and SOUL-utions that it has for you. The purity of your heart within Love is the greatest engine of spiritual wealth creation. The Universal Law of Divine Compensation represents the natural workings of the Universe, but you can block it and deactivate the Law with unloving, judgmental, and scarcity thoughts, feelings, and beliefs.

Putting Love first opens you up to the miracles of the Universe. The Universe can provide you with the transformation that is necessary for any situation or with any lack mentality. It's about you making the Conscious Choice to heal that which is within you and takes you out of alignment with Love and your Soul's Essence.

As you come into alignment with thoughts and feelings of Infinite Love, you can become sovereign unto yourself. You can also transform the lower thought forms and beliefs of the collective and current world status. There is nothing the Universe can't provide you once you create the vibrational alignment and match to what you desire and what's in your Highest Order.

What are your True loving thoughts, feelings, and beliefs about yourself and others? Remember the Universal Law of Harmony. You can harmonize with the abundance of the Universe as you stay in Love and your heart-centered power.

Here are some qualities of BE-ing and feeling abundant: plentiful, copious, ample, profuse, rich, lavish, opulent, generous, bountiful, over-flowing, prolific, large, expansive, and Infinite.

You have the Conscious Choice to embody these qualities and claim "I AM Abundant!" In this, you are your ALL ... Abundant (Absolute) Light & Love!

A Message from the Council of ALL

Greeting Dear Ones,

Do you know how much abundance there is within the Universe? In the vastness of the Universe, the Infinite exists, and it is yours for the asking.

And, to receive it, there must be a willingness to allow yourself to receive without the need to prove that you are worthy or deserving of the abundant blessings we desire to bestow upon you.

We know you have been taught "it is better to give than to receive." This is actually not true. It is important to give and receive in equal measure. This is how harmony and balance are maintained. This is how flow is main-tained and becomes sustainable and expansive.

We invite you to bring the feelings and the vibrations of abundance within your Physical Bodies, while infusing it within your Energy Centers (your Chakras) and Energy Bodies. We invite you to think and feel in abundant terms and vibrations.

This can shift you into a new level of consciousness ... Abundant Prosperity. We invite you to say, feel, think, and believe I AM Abundant! on a daily basis. We invite you to have this become your new state of BE-ing and consciousness. Claim and accept this as your Divine birthright because it is.

We love you so. Blessed Be.

Gem/Crystal for the Principle: Pyrite

Pyrite is a symbol of good luck and fortune, commonly referred to as 'fool's gold' and known as the High Manifester. It is the abundance stone and is helpful in attracting money.

It can be used for grounding and for opening your heart to allow more prosperity in many ways, and especially in financial terms.

Pyrite is great to have if you are in business; keep a small stone inside your wallet, purse, or cash drawer, and one on your desk or in your workspace. It is also a 'get-it-done' stone and helps with your creativity and productivity.

It vibrates to #3: joy, creativity, power, lifeforce, and the trinity effect.

The Universal Law of Giving

The Universal Law of Giving is giving and receiving as a part of the exchange that perpetuates the energy flow of the Universe. As you are receptive to the premise of giving that which you desire to receive, the abundance of the Universe is perpetuated in your life. You must give to receive, and you must receive in order to give.

The energy of each is equal, and the Universe will respond to either, along with a pull of the energy of the other. The Universe operates through dynamic exchange; giving and receiving are different aspects of the flow of energy in the Universe. And, in your willingness to give that which you seek, you keep the abundance of the Universe circulating in your life.

Wherever you go, and whoever you encounter, bring them a gift. The gift may be a compliment, a flower, an object, or a blessing. Give something to everyone you meet ... this begins the process of circulating Love, joy, wealth, and affluence in your own life and in the lives of others.

Gratefully receive all the gifts that life has to offer you. Practice this by receiving and being grateful for the gifts of nature, such as the sunlight, the sound of birds singing, the flowers, the spring showers, or the first snow of winter.

Be open to receive from others, whether it be in the form of Love and appreciation, a compliment or accolade, material gift, money, or even a prayer and healing energies. If you don't, you stop the flow.

Make a commitment to keep wealth circulating in your life by giving and receiving life's most precious gifts: the gifts of kindness, caring, affection, appreciation, and most of all, Love. Each time you meet someone, silently wish them joy, peace, prosperity, laughter, and whatever else you feel they need, want, or would Love to receive.

The Universe will thank you with a continuous flow of Abundant Prosperity as it knows it can count on you to spread the Love!

The Universal Law of Abundance

The Universal Law of Abundance is sometimes referred to as the Law of Opulence or Success. By creating visualizations of abundance in your life, you can draw this energy of success into your reality. Success or abundance does not *only* apply to money. There is success in living your life fully, your spirituality, your health and well-being, ways of communication, being in heart-centered relationships, and so on.

When creating the abundance of financial gain, remember to be *in* this world (3rd Dimension physical manifestations) but not of this world. Your possessions or bank account do not represent the sum total of who you are.

Within the Universe, abundant Infinite resources exist and its possibilities and resources flow through the energies of giving and receiving. If you need or want something (or someone), then create space within your life, so you are ready to receive it. The Universe will recognize the opening and your willingness to receive and fill it with abundance.

As you transcend any fear of scarcity or not enough, or even the need to hold onto things (or people), hoarding, or greed, giving and receiving within your life experience will come into balance. Thus, you move into a 'state of abundance.'

In a state of abundance, you have the experience of having more than enough, and even that of surplus and overflow. As such, you have all that you need and want. You can fulfill your Soul's purpose with the assurance that the Universe is supporting you as you continue to expand your state of Abundant Prosperity consciousness. This requires the complete balance of giving and receiving in which lack, scarcity, or hoarding are NOT experienced.

The imbalance of giving and receiving causes the experience and feelings of lack, scarcity, and/or hoarding within one's life. *Lack* is the result of giving without receiving. *Scarcity* is the result of believing there is limited supply. *Hoarding* is the result of receiving and holding onto things (and even money) without giving. All of these reflect a non-trust that there's enough for All and that the Universe is abundant.

Upon the physical earth plane, so much time and energy has become devoted to sustaining one's lifestyle. As such, it has detracted from the actual purpose of why a Soul incarnates into physical form. A Soul incarnates to spiritually evolve, to experience life in a Physical Body, and to fulfill its Divine purpose.

When so much of your life is devoted to making a living, there's little energy or time available for spiritual evolution. Much of the time is expended in the pursuits of monetary gain, which often is the result of inflated expectations of financial success, or a lifestyle that doesn't really support your spiritual endeavors. It is for this reason that devotion to your spiritual evolution may need to preclude (or be adjusted) in your desire for wealth, or an exorbitant lifestyle.

On the other side of the pendulum swing, there are also those upon the spiritual path who believe that they must give everything away in order to be considered devoted and to fulfill their purpose. With this belief system, one will continually create lack and not enough to even pay one's bills.

To transcend a belief in lack, or an erroneous belief around money and what it means, you must also learn how to allow yourself to receive full compensation for all that you give. This is a part of Divine Compensation.

You came here for a reason, allow yourself to be supported in fulfilling your purpose. This includes financially.

The Universe is your Source *and* it flows through people investing in what you offer or sell, and even those who gift money or resources to you. When you accept their money, you're helping them fulfill their agreements (which may have been made in other lifetimes or even before they incarnated) and their purpose to help you. This is done by accepting what they pay you or offer to you.

With balanced giving and receiving, the amount charged for a particular service must be aligned with the energy expended in the service offered. The person who is charging must be in vibrational alignment with their fees as well so there is congruency for both parties, and it flows with ease and grace.

All energetic exchanges in giving and receiving must be in equal balance, or karma ends up being accrued by one or both parties. If too much is charged, karma is accrued. If too little or nothing is charged, karma is again accrued.

Within the 5th Dimension and beyond, it is not an either/or, it is an AND … spiritual evolution AND wealth on all levels. It is your Divine Compensation to live a prosperous and abundant life!

My Abundant Exploration

◊   Where in my life do I feel Abundant, and where do I not?

◊   What does abundance mean to me and how do I determine if I AM Abundant?

◊   Do I have beliefs of lack, not enough, or scarcity?

◊   In what areas of my life does lack/scarcity/not enough consciousness show up!

◊   How does it play out in my life, health, relationships, finances, and career or business?

◊   What are the results due to these beliefs?

◊   Am I open to receive? If not, why?

◊   Are there any blocks to me receiving?

◊   If I over give (and over do), what are the reasons for it?

◊   Where do I not allow the balance of giving and receiving?

◊   What are my beliefs about being both spiritual AND wealthy? Is there an either/or in my beliefs?

◊   Am I willing to believe and claim, "I AM Abundant!"? If not, why?

The Abundant Elevation Protocol

The Abundant Protocol includes the Abundant Elevation Code within the *CCC ... Clear, Cleanse, and Calibrate* portion of the Protocol as well as the Elevation Codes of Freedom, Forgiveness, and Love.

This assists you to let go of the patterns, thoughts, feelings, and beliefs regarding lack, scarcity, and feelings that you don't have enough, or are enough. This energy can permeate any area of your life, relationships, health, finances, and business, with the sense you don't have enough Love, energy, money, food, clients, resources, time, etc.

It can also help you to release the beliefs of you are not enough, or you're not good enough. With this Elevation Protocol and Codes, you can move from the *lack* to the *MORE*, then to the *ALL*.

The Abundant Elevation Code can help shift your lack mentality and scarcity consciousness to an Abundant Prosperity consciousness which then can elevate you into Unity consciousness. It's important to identify your family beliefs systems and programming from society, religions, and cultures about money, resources, and wealth. Look at what you took on as yours, what's True for you now, and what you want to shift.

The *EEE ... Energize, Elevate, and Evolve* portion of the Abundant Protocol includes the Love, Harmony, Trust, Abundant, and Prosperity Elevation Codes. We've reviewed all of the Elevation Codes except Abundant in the previous chapters.

As you go into the *EEE* portion of the Abundant Protocol, claim your Divine birthright to be in the flow of Abundant Prosperity and raise your vibrations and consciousness so you are open to receiving your ALL!

The Prosperity and Thrive Protocols and Elevation Codes in Chapters Eleven and Twelve respectively are excellent to combine with this Abundant Protocol. Plus, the Trust Protocol can assist you as well, so you trust the Universe to support you; you really believe that the Universe has your back and is always advocating for you.

We suggest reviewing them, so you can elevate your ability to attract and receive. This also assists you to Truly claim "I AM Abundant!" And, to elevate and evolve into more of your ALL ... Abundant Light & Love!

The Abundant Protocol Features
The Elevation Code of Abundant

Gratitude
(Silver)   *Receive*

Abundant Elevation Code includes the Diamond Co-Creation Codes of
Gratitude (with the Silver Band) and Receive

It is important to have gratitude for the past, present, and future. Gratitude is the Highest vibration to access Love and flow of Abundant Prosperity. The Abundant Elevation Code offers a creative and powerful life force with Universal Intelligence which can assist you to open, recognize, and receive inspired, joyful Infinite Possibilities and SOUL-utions.

The Gratitude Code assists in harmonizing and optimizing 12th Chakra — Universal Source Connection. It helps you connect with Divine Source and Universal Source energy, and access your advanced spiritual skills beyond what you currently know. The 12th Chakra helps you tap into Unity consciousness, and it also assists you with your ascension process to transform your human body into more of your Diamond 'Light' Body.

Within the Abundant Elevation Code, the Receive Code amplifies the gratitude you hold and express. The more grateful you are, the more you receive. And, as you receive more, you ideally become even more grateful. There is a more easeful and graceful flow into the ALL as gratitude radiates throughout you and around you.

The Receive Code assists your Third Eye — 6th Chakra and Gravitational Energy Body. You can access the Infinite by connecting with and listening to the guidance of your intuition to receive ideas, information, and visions from your Soul and the Divine … the Universal Mind and Higher consciousness. You can receive more Universal Source energies, and with your Soul's wisdom, utilize it to create your Highest Order and Infinite Diamond Potential.

Remember, the Gravitational Body helps you to attract and repel energies, opportunities, resources, people, and experiences. It goes out of energetic alignment when another Energy Body is compromised and out of balance. When you feel you're not attracting what you Truly desire, always check to see if your Gravitational Body is in alignment with Love, your Highest Order, and fullest Potential.

If it is out of alignment, your Gravitational Body can actually repel your desires and attract what ends up becoming a lesson and a growth opportunity for you. When it's aligned, it repels the experiences you no longer need to encounter, so that's the good news! In addition, when your Gravitational Body is aligned, it's easier for you to attract and receive your abundance and what you want.

The Silver Band encircles both the Gratitude and Receive Codes and assists you to receive with more ease and grace; it helps you to co-create with the Universe. The Silver offers the Feminine energy of receptivity and encourages the expression of who you Truly are and your emotions … *energy in motion.* It enhances your intuitive abilities and connection with the Universe and helps you to maintain balance between the spiritual and the physical. It also harmonizes your inner life rhythms with the cycles of nature.

The Abundant Elevation Code opens the doorways to allow yourself to receive your ALL! And, by implementing the Universal Laws of Giving and Abundance with the Code, you can find yourself in the vibrations of wealth at any given time.

Activating the Abundant and Prosperity Elevation Codes on a daily basis helps you to align with an Abundant Prosperity consciousness. And, utilizing the Abundant and Prosperity Protocols together accelerates your process into this Higher consciousness. It is suggested to work with one or both Protocols 2-3 times a week as you work with their 5th Dimension Principles.

The Abundant Protocol … I AM Abundant!

(see next page)

The Abundant Protocol ... 1 AM Abundant!

The Elevation Codes	The Diamond Co-Creation Codes	Code's (S) Spiritual #	Code's (M) Mental #	Code's (P) Projection #	Purposes
CCC					The Past & The Old
Freedom	Expression & Power	8	9	8	Release, Clear, Cleanse, Transmute & Calibrate
Forgiveness	Compassion & Foundation	9	3	3	Release, Clear, Cleanse, Transmute & Calibrate
Love	Compassion & Connection	3	9	3	Release, Clear, Cleanse, Transmute & Calibrate
Abundant	Gratitude (Silver) & Receive	8	2	1	Release, Clear, Cleanse, Transmute & Calibrate
EEE					5D – 5th Dimension
Love	Compassion & Connection	3	9	3	Energize, Elevate & Evolve into the 5D
Harmony	Receive & Wisdom	3	8	11	Energize, Elevate & Evolve into the 5D
Trust	Receive & Manifest	6	4	1	Energize, Elevate & Evolve into the 5D
Abundant	Gratitude (Silve) & Receive	8	2	1	Energize, Elevate & Evolve into the 5D
Prosperity	Connection & Anchor	4	1	5	Energize, Elevate & Evolve into the 5D

This is only recommended verbiage. If you're guided to say something different, then do so. The Codes 'know' exactly what you need and want so you can't do it wrong.

CCC: (Name of Elevation Codes) Activate, Activate, Activate, Clear, Cleanse, and Calibrate, Calibrate, Calibrate, 44 Times Divine Source Speed at the 44th Power to Purify, Purify, Purify, my Chakras and Energy Bodies, so I AM in the state of BE-ing abundant within the 5th Dimension or Beyond for my Highest Order and Infinite Diamond Potential.

Violet Flame … Transmute, Transmute, Transmute, 33 Times Divine Source Speed at the 33rd Power.

EEE: (Name of Elevation Codes) Energize, Energize, Energize, Elevate, Elevate, Elevate, Evolve, Evolve, Evolve 44 Times Divine Source Speed at the 44th Power and saturate every cell of my Being to embody "I AM Abundant" and attract my Abundant Prosperity with ease and grace within the 5th Dimension to fulfill my Highest Order and Infinite Diamond Potential.

Resources from
Co-Create Your Success

We hope this book has been inspiring and led you to a new way of BE-ing and DO-ing within the 5th Dimension, so you embody more Love, joy, and prosperity in any and all aspects of your life, relationships, health and well-being, spirituality, finances, and career or business. As you integrate these insights, we invite you to take your transformation and evolution further.

Our signature programs, built around The Diamond Co-Creative System® (what many of our clients call their "Soul-Aligned Success System"), are designed to take you from where you are to where you are meant to be. It takes you to your next level and creates the abilities to live the life you desire to manifest.

If you believe you're here to make a difference ... we take you from uncertainty to success to significance. Whether you are seeking clarity and confidence, leadership expansion, or a deeper sense of fulfillment in life or business, these programs provide proven, step-by-step frameworks to unlock your next level of impact, influence, and abundance.

Here's how you can continue your journey and step fully into your ALL:

YOUR PATH OF EVOLUTION BEGINS HERE ...

Embarking on a journey toward Soul-aligned success requires the right tools and support. Whether you're ready to deepen your connection with your True essence, expand into the life you're meant to live, or create a greater positive impact in the world, these programs will guide you every step of the way.

DIAMOND CODE CLUB
Awaken Your Fullest Potential

Your energy shapes your reality. The Diamond Code Club is designed for those who are ready to heal the past, step into the authentic expression of who you are, and create unshakable confidence in what you want to do. It utilizes the Diamond Co-Creation Codes to activate your fullest Potential and to create the life you want to live.

What you'll experience:
* Monthly activations to shift limitations and blocks to expand your ability to move into possibilities.
* Practical tools to help you trust your intuition and take decisive action toward fulfilling your visions.
* A supportive community to help keep you energetically aligned, empowered, and inspired as you grow.

You don't have to figure it out alone — The Code Club is here for you. Shift your energy and move into a life of Love, joy, peace, passion, purpose, and so much more!

Join the Diamond Code Club today ➤
https://link.cocreateyoursuccess.com/eiyabookdiamondcodeclub

A 30-DAY SOUL'S JOURNEY
Daily Activations to Create Transformations

In just 30 days, you can break free from old limitations, reconnect with your Soul's purpose and plan, and start creating life on your own terms. This guided experience offers the structure, support, and Soul level clarity you've been seeking.

What You'll Experience:
* Daily guidance that's infused with the power of the Diamond Co-Creation Codes to shift your energy and perspective.
* Sacred meditations and music activations to awaken your inner wisdom and amplify your abilities to manifest what you envision.

◆ A deeper understanding of what your Soul wants you to know, so you can align your actions with your greater purpose and Potential.

This isn't just another course — it's a portal to move into the expansion of YOU. If you're ready to break through, your Soul is ready to guide you!

Begin your 30-Day Soul's Journey today ➵
https://link.cocreateyoursuccess.com/eiya30daysoulsjourney

EVOLVE YOUR ALL
5TH DIMENSION MENTORSHIP
Go to Your Next Level with Ease, Grace & Joy

You've felt the pull toward something greater — now it's time to step fully into it. This immersive mentorship is designed for those who refuse to settle and those who are ready to elevate every aspect of their lives — relationships, health, spirituality, wealth, contribution, and career or business success.

What You'll Experience:
◆ Master the 5th Dimension Principles & Elevation Codes from The Diamond Co-Creative System® to shift into effortless flow, abundance, and alignment.
◆ Two 5-Month Transformational Series per year, guiding you to sustain deep healing, personal expansion, and next-level manifestation.
◆ A powerful container for growth, support, and activation so you can prosper and thrive in all areas of life.

This isn't about incremental change — this is about stepping into your ALL. If you're ready to operate within a Higher frequency, to play full on in life and business, and to unlock the limitless possibilities waiting for you …

Join the 5th Dimension Mentorship today ➵
https://link.cocreateyoursuccess.com/
eiyabook5thdimensionmentorship

DIAMOND LIGHT CIRCLE
Master Mind. Master Heart. Master Soul.
From Success to Significance!

You are not here to play small. You are here to master your gifts, amplify your contribution, and co-create at the Highest level. We invite you to incorporate your Soul's Essence and purpose, and uplevel the connection of your spirituality in who you are and what you do.

The Diamond Light Circle is an exclusive, yearlong experience for visionaries, executives, entrepreneurs, leaders, legacy builders, and seekers who are ready to transcend limitations, embody your fullest Potential, and leave a lasting legacy in ways that you want to create positive influence and impact.

What You'll Experience:

- Master Mind. Master Heart. Master Soul. Step into an intimate, High frequency circle where you'll be supported, expanded, and activated at every level.
- Energy Mastery with the Ascension Principles & Codes from The Diamond Co-Creative System®. Learn to harness the power of Higher consciousness to create success, fulfillment, and freedom on your terms.
- A legacy-driven approach to transformation. Move beyond success into deep significance as you embody and align your leadership, purpose, and contribution with your Soul's vision.

Your next level of evolution is calling. Are you ready to answer the beckoning of your Soul?

Step into the Diamond Light Circle today ➤
https://link.cocreateyoursuccess.com/eiyabookdiamondlightcircle

THE DIAMOND CO-CREATIVE SYSTEM®
ACCREDITATION FOR COACHES,
PRACTITIONERS & TEACHERS
Make a Bigger Difference for Your Clients!

You are a unique expression of your Soul's wisdom, passion, and purpose. You are here for a reason. The Diamond Co-Creative System® can help you to further discover and develop your gifts, skills, and knowledge through its Accreditation program. Then, you can share the System with others through your channeling, coaching, mentoring, healing, and transformation within your own practice and business.

The benefits of incorporating The Diamond Co-Creative System® into your business and creating your own legacy are …

- The System is a leading-edge proven technology with turnkey tools and techniques that help you to positively position yourself to make a difference in someone's life.
- It gives you a powerful point of differentiation, enabling you to stand out amongst the crowd of coaches and practitioners as you step fully into your power and leadership to serve others in the Highest Order.
- The System does not compete with any other modality, or spiritual practice, you currently use … it will only enhance them and help you to assist others with even more powerful tools and techniques.

The end results — by including The Diamond Co-Creative System® as a modality within your business and contribution to the world, it can help you build a sustainable and thriving practice as you co-create success within yourself and with others!

Be the difference today ➼
https://link.cocreateyoursuccess.com/eiyabookdccsaccreditation

FREE EVENTS, RESOURCES & TOOLS TO ELEVATE & EXPEDITE YOUR JOURNEY

Experience Transformation—On Your Time, In Your Way.

- **Quarterly Free Virtual Events:** Dive into powerful teachings and activations from The Diamond Co-Creative System®, designed to help you expand, align, and evolve.

- **Workshops & Retreats:** Join Amanda for immersive, High-frequency experiences held live two to three times a year — where deep healing meets quantum breakthroughs and activations into your MORE!

- **Online Courses & Self-Guided Programs:** Access transformational teachings anytime, anywhere.

  Explore the full library at ↠
  https://link.cocreateyoursuccess.com/eiyabooksoulutions.

CLAIM YOUR FREE GIFTS!

- *Evolve Into Your ALL* **Book Resource Hub:** A full-size color set of the High vibrational toolset of the Elevation Codes and other resources to deepen your practice and assist you in your expansion. One of the resources is the *T.A.M.E. Your Life with The Universal 'L'* free e-Book which includes the different colors of the Universal 'L's and how to further use them.

  Download yours today ↠
  https://link.cocreateyoursuccess.com/eiyabookresourcehub

- *Manifest Your ALL!* **e-Book:** Includes the Universal Manifestation Template and proven methods to call in your desires — without wasting time, money, or energy.

  Get started today to manifest your visions ↠
  https://link.cocreateyoursuccess.com/eiyabookmyagift

- **Free Co-Dependency Survey:** Is co-dependency 'running' the show and holding you back? Uncover hidden patterns that get in your way and shift into empowerment. Receive an in-depth report to help you become aware of your patterns so you can make the choice to resolve them once and for all.

  Take the survey today ➤
  https://link.cocreateyoursuccess.com/eiyabookcodependencysurvey

- **Connect with Amanda:** Book a free Create Your ALL! 20-minute consultation with Amanda. She works with seekers, visionaries, entrepreneurs, executives, and legacy-driven leaders — who want to align their success with fulfillment and Soul's purpose. If you're ready to uplevel your life and business and step into unshakable confidence, meaning, and significance with limitless potential, then connect with Amanda.

  Book your call with Amanda ➤
  https://link.cocreateyoursuccess.com/createyourallfreeconsultation

BE SOCIAL WITH US & FOLLOW US!

Facebook: https://www.facebook.com/cocreateyoursuccess/
Instagram: https://www.instagram.com/cocreateyoursuccess/
LinkedIn: www.linkedin.com/in/amandaslade
YouTube: https://www.youtube.com/@cocreateyoursuccess

OTHER CO-CREATE YOUR SUCCESS LINKS

Email: Support@CoCreateYourSuccess.com
Website: https://cocreateyoursuccess.com

About The Author

For over 20 years, Amanda Slade successfully climbed the corporate ladder within the competitive industries of cosmetics and fragrance in high-level managerial roles, as well as in pharmaceutical marketing as a Vice President of Marketing & Sales for a New York publishing firm — yet deep unfulfillment lingered, and she knew she was meant for more. That inner calling from her Soul led her on a transformational journey to heal the past, awaken her spirit, and create the legacy she was destined to build.

Today, Amanda is the creator of The Diamond Co-Creative System®, a revolutionary technology and approach that integrates spiritual wisdom and Sacred Geometry with practical strategies to deliver tangible, real-life results. While bridging science and spirituality, she helps women to reconnect to themselves and others, access their brilliance, and co-create purposeful success with lasting significance. Many clients refer to the System as the "Soul-Aligned Success System" which provides a roadmap to elevate them to new heights of realizing their greatest potential with a new sense of fulfillment and inner peace.

Since 2001, Amanda has worked with thousands of women — seekers, visionaries, entrepreneurs, executives, and legacy-driven leaders — to break free from fears and invisible barriers, reclaim their power and passion, and redefine success on their own terms. Her clients move from overworking, exhaustion, self-doubt, next-step uncertainty, and lack of fulfillment to clarity, confidence, and meaning without sacrificing themselves in the process. They transition from uncertainty to empowerment, from career to calling, from success to significance, from leadership to legacy.

Amanda believes true success does not require choosing between achievement and fulfillment or between a thriving career or business and a balanced life. Through intuitive leadership, energy realignment, and next-level life and business strategies, she shows women how to increase their impact, influence, and income by leading authentically and living in alignment with who they truly are. Amanda guides women to shift from striving for success to creating a meaningful life, business, and legacy — one that reflects their deepest values and greatest gifts.

A bestselling author, sought-after speaker, and expert in Strategic Spirituality, Amanda is featured in *Pillars of Power* alongside Dr. Joe Vitale, John Assaraf, Mark Victor Hansen, and other luminaries from *The Secret*. Because Amanda knows success alone isn't enough, she is known to help women move beyond success — into lives of profound purpose, freedom, and legacy led by their Soul's calling.

Grounded

BALANCE

Gratitude (Gold)

Power

FREEDOM

Expression

Anchor

JOY

Compassion

Power

PASSION

Creation

Grace
(Gold)

PEACE

Foundation

Anchor

PROSPERITY

Connection

Wisdom

SOUL

Grace
(Silver)

Creation

THRIVE

Foundation

www.ingramcontent.com/pod-product-compliance
Lightning Source LLC
Chambersburg PA
CBHW060143150626
46550CB00014B/441